For centuries Ort[...] but in recent dec[...] theologians from R[...] [Bol]sheviks and the rapid growth of population mobility and communications, this situation has changed.

As an evangelical pastor and theologian in Athens, Giotis Kantartzis addresses the strengths of Orthodox theology together with the equally evident obstacles that it poses for evangelical and Reformed Christians. Blessed with wide learning, acute theological insight, and pastoral experience from living in an Orthodox country, Dr. Kantartzis is outstandingly qualified for this task, which he does superbly.

Robert Letham
Professor of Systematic and Historical Theology,
Union School of Theology, Wales

This book reminds us that the differences between Evangelical Protestantism and Eastern Orthodoxy are rooted in fundamental principles that touch on every aspect of theology. The presentation is clear and fair to both sides, making it a reliable resource for dialogue between these two very different Christian traditions.

Gerald Bray
Research Professor of Divinity, Beeson Divinity School,
Birmingham, Alabama

Kantartzis offers a unique book that combines careful and sensitive analysis of Orthodox Christianity with a respectful and constructive engagement from the perspective of his own Evangelical faith. His thoughtful responses to various themes as expressed by contemporary Orthodox theologians are grounded in an authentic listening that demonstrates an openness to being challenged by Orthodox theology. Kantartzis has accomplished nothing less than providing a book that is not simply informative, but is itself a performance of authentic dialogue.

Aristotle Papanikolaou
Professor of Theology and the Archbishop Demetrios
Chair in Orthodox Theology and Culture,
Fordham University, New York
Co-founding Director, Orthodox Christian Studies Center

Don't judge a book by its page-count. In a relatively brief compass, Pastor Kantartzis covers the most important points with clear, concise and well-researched prose. This book proves that other views can be treated fairly, summarized without polemical distortion, and only then critiqued from an evangelical perspective. Besides reading the main sources, living in a culture shaped by Orthodoxy equips Pastor Kantartzis to explain a very non-Western form of Christianity to Westerners. If you want the best engagement with Orthodoxy from an evangelical perspective, look no further.

Michael Horton
J. G. Machen Professor of Systematic Theology and
Apologetics, Westminster Seminary, Escondido, California

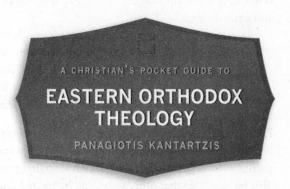

A CHRISTIAN'S POCKET GUIDE TO

EASTERN ORTHODOX THEOLOGY

PANAGIOTIS KANTARTZIS

An Evangelical Perspective

CHRISTIAN
FOCUS

Copyright © Panagiotis Kantartzis 2021

paperback ISBN 978-1-5271-0641-3
epub ISBN 978-1-5271-0706-9
mobi ISBN 978-1-5271-0707-6

10 9 8 7 6 5 4 3 2 1
Published in 2021
by
Christian Focus Publications Ltd,
Geanies House, Fearn, Ross-shire,
IV20 1TW, Scotland, Great Britain
www.christianfocus.com

Cover design by Daniel Van Straaten

Printed by Nørhaven

CONTENTS

⚠ Warning

✎ Don't Forget

⑦ Stop and Think

✳ Point of Interest

INTRODUCTION

Several excellent books already in print introduce Eastern Orthodox theology to a western, and specifically an evangelical, audience. Of particular note are those by Donald Fairbairn[1] and Robert Letham.[2] This book presupposes these prior works, and constitutes a modest attempt, not so much to present Orthodox theology, but chiefly to interact with it and respond to it from an evangelical viewpoint.

I must stress that I will not engage with the full gamut of the Orthodox Church and the orthodox way, but rather with its theology, and even there I shall not address every one of its component parts. I shall only deal with matters that lie at its core, and this only in a cursory way due to the size limitations of this publication. As I hope we shall see, theology is not made up of individual doctrines but entails a system, a mosaic where each part holds together with all the other parts. I have chosen these specific parts because they provide a basic outline of Orthodox theology.

The purpose of this book is to outline with accuracy, to converse with charity, and to provide a sincere response, always having the intention to explain the protestant position, but also to challenge the evangelical reader to reflection, and indeed also the orthodox reader. It is therefore a book that is directed at an evangelical readership but with a desire to include orthodox believers in the conversation. If the previous books were attempting to present the orthodox way to Evangelicals, the hope for this book is for orthodox believers to discover an evangelical response to the various positions held by their theology.

At this point, I must clarify two things. The first is that the theology of textbooks and the academy does not always align with the theology of the laity. My purpose is to interact chiefly with the first group, bearing in mind that this may not reflect the popular ideas of the wider orthodox community. At the same time, I have not learnt about Orthodoxy through books or in the context of an orthodox community of the diaspora somewhere in the West but through living in a traditional orthodox majority country. The occasion for my interaction with Orthodox theology was not a lingering curiosity or an

In what ways might the theology of the laity differ from the theology of textbooks in a majority orthodox country?

attraction to some seemingly exotic ideas. It was born out of a life of pastoring and witnessing in this environment.

The second point to clarify concerns the term, 'evangelical'. As we approach Orthodoxy it is crucial to recognise the vast spectrum of views and nuances within Protestantism. The specific 'location' of someone within the broad spectrum of Protestantism plays a significant role in the way he or she assesses Orthodoxy. My own position and the standpoint from which I am interacting with Orthodox theology it can be described as broadly Evangelical[3] and more particularly Reformed.[4]

Each chapter follows the same format. I begin with a basic presentation of the orthodox thinking on a particular subject. Here the reader may note that there are several long quotations from the writings of Orthodox theologians. That is because it is always better to let someone speak for himself or herself. Then I proceed to engage in dialogue with this position. This dialogue includes a positive appraisal of various aspects of the orthodox view, as truly encountering the 'other' can enrich us, since we may discover helpful elements that we had never noticed before. I then continue by commenting on points of divergence. For a dialogue to be both meaningful and engaging, it must have theses, followed by the formulation and elaboration of antitheses. At the end there is usually an attempt to reframe the evangelical position in light of the preceding interaction with the orthodox view.

As I have already noted, my approach is not intended to be polemical but sincere. Our purpose is not to crush an opponent but to better understand a brother or sister, and why not, even to help them understand.

Panagiotis Kantartzis
Athens, 2020

1

THE MODE OF THEOLOGISING:

MYSTERY & APOPHATICISM

O Trinity,
   beyond being, beyond divinity, beyond goodness
   and guide of Christians in divine wisdom,
     direct us to the mystical summits
     more than unknown and beyond light.
There are the simple, absolved,
   and unchanged mysteries of theology
   lie hidden in the darkness beyond light
Of the hidden mystical silence,
   there, in the greatest darkness,
   that beyond all that is most evident
   exceedingly illuminates the sightless intellects.[5]

The above text is found at the beginning of the Mystical Theology of Dionysius the Areopagite. We begin by looking at this prayer since it is important to understand the distinctive 'mode' of doing theology in the orthodox tradition before looking at its content.

Apophatic theology describes God by what He is not (negative statements), in contrast to cataphatic theology, which describes Him by what He is (positive statements).

THE ORTHODOX WAY

The beginning of theological contemplation is not to be found in theological handbooks or even in creedal formulations. Theology does not concern knowledge apprehended by the mind but a participation in the truth, which must be attained through prayer and the liturgical life of the Church. Andrew Louth, commenting on an extract from Maximus the Confessor's commentary on the Lord's Prayer, says, 'The way in which St Maximus understands theology is striking here. First, the mysteries of theology are mediated by a prayer, not by a creed or a treatise: we only understand by participating ourselves in prayer.'[6] As he explains more fully elsewhere, one does not enter into the truth through rational engagement, but through prayer. This truth is not articulated but accessed through 'inarticulateness', through the silence.[7]

How then do we theologise? According to Louth, doctrines 'are not truths which could be appraised and understood outside the bosom of the Church', but 'they are part of the church's reflection on the mystery of her life with God'.[8] For this reason, the mode of theologising is 'primarily through participation in the divine liturgy, for it is here that the truths that we confess are not just brought to mind, but in some way enacted so that we can take part.'[9]

This mode is defined by the subject matter of 'theology'. As Lossky, following Dionysius the Aeropagite,[10] maintains in his classic work, *The Mystical Theology of the Eastern Church*:

> If in seeing God one can know what one sees, then one has not seen God in Himself but something intelligible, something which is inferior to Him. It is by unknowing (ἀγνωσία) that one may know Him who is above every possible object of knowledge. Proceeding by negations one ascends from the inferior degrees of being to the highest, by progressively setting aside all that can be known, in order to draw near to the Unknown in the darkness of absolute ignorance.[11]

When surveying the typical Icon of the Transfiguration of the Lord, an event of particular importance for apophatic theology, we see the light of Mount Tabor radiating out from a centre that has been painted completely black. From that darkness a light shines forth, with the rays falling on the disciples. Of note here is the fact that Dionysius, in his Mystical Theology, speaks of 'ray of divine light' (1.1).

At the end of this ascent[12] of 'theologising', we do not find 'understanding' or 'perception' but union with God, usually expressed by the term, 'theosis'. Lossky writes, 'unknowability does not mean agnosticism or refusal to know God. Nevertheless, this knowledge will only be attained in the way which leads not to knowledge but to union—to deification.'[13] This mode of theologizing is often referred to as 'apophatic', in contrast to 'cataphatic'.

AN EVANGELICAL RESPONSE

It is worth noting several helpful aspects of this approach. First of all, the emphasis on the connection between theology on the one hand and worship and prayer on the other is a much needed reminder for other traditions, which tend to turn theology into a cold, academic discipline. Theology is intimately connected to the life of the church and is above all doxological and eucharistic. Something that indeed the early church confessed and lived out (*lex orandi, lex credendi*—the law of prayer is the law of belief). It is also important to take to heart the Orthodox emphasis that knowledge about God is not to be sought as an end in itself but always with the final goal of knowing God Himself and, more specifically, of being united with Him. Theology, therefore, is an ecclesiastical, doxological and even soteriological pursuit, as it pertains to a 'knowledge' that is personal and experiential.

Finally, it is good to be reminded of the limits of the theological endeavour. All too often, the mode of theologising in the West is characterised by a scholastic and rationalistic approach, which gives the impression that it is possible to place God under a microscope and analyse Him.

Nonetheless, as A.N. Williams has rightly observed, 'Both moderate and radical apophaticism require a lot of explaining if they are to be reconciled with any Christian theology that insists on the primacy of the Bible',[14] which is exactly what evangelical theology insists on. Is silence the only alternative to flippant God-talk? Lossky speaks of the 'margin of silence' as the authentic context of theology.[15] Silence, however, is vague, potentially entailing anything from nothing to everything.

In the prayer referenced at the beginning of this chapter, we see Dionysius praying to the Trinity to lead him to the summit where he may encounter the mysteries of theology, hidden in the 'silence' of 'darkness'. This idea holds special significance for the apophatic way, since it is connected with the paradigmatic image of Moses' ascent up to Sinai, where he meets God in the darkness. Here of course, we must respond with the fact that, according to the Biblical narrative, although Moses ascends Sinai in order to meet God, he then descends having received ten 'words' from God. This underlines the essential role

---

Despite praying to encounter the mysteries hidden in the 'silence,' Dionysius is anything but silent as he proceeds to write about God. Here, Calvin's famous criticism of Dionysius is relevant. After describing Dionysius' Celestial Hierarchy as impressive at first but turning out to be 'nothing but talk', he then makes the comment, 'If you read that book, you would think a man fallen from heaven recounted not what he had learned but what he had seen with his own eyes' (*Institutes*, 1.14.4).

that Scripture, understood as God's words, plays in the way that God connects with us. According to the writer of Hebrews, 'Long ago, at many times and in many ways, God spoke to our fathers by the prophets, but in these last days he has spoken to us by his Son' (1:1-2). These verses emphasise the fact that God's communication with us is both verbal and personal, through words and the Word. We speak of God, in other words we theologise, because God first spoke to us. Thus, even Dionysius repeatedly makes clear that his words about God are drawn from God's own words, revealed in Scripture.[16] At this point, it is useful to juxtapose the conception of mystery that we encounter in apophatic theology with the 'mystery' that we encounter in the pages of the New Testament. In the New Testament, 'mystery' is associated with the idea of revelation and disclosure (i.e. 1 Tim 3:16). The essence of mystery, in this context, is that it is not annulled in the event of disclosure. In other words, it is not an 'enigma', that is somehow resolved when the truth is revealed. The 'mystery' remains a mystery. What, however, does this

According to A.N. Williams, Dionysius himself affirms that we speak of God because He first speaks to us. In his treatise 'On the Divine Names', Dionysius states that 'to the extent that the ray of the godhead freely gives of itself, we are drawn inward toward greater splendours by a temperance and piety for what is divine' (I,1 588A). Williams notes that, 'if you want to attain to something beyond yourself, you must get your notions of it from the source, from that which lies beyond' (A.N. Williams, 'The Transcendence of Apophaticism', 322). In other words, we may speak of Him who is beyond all description if we have something that is 'here', but this must come from the 'beyond'.

mean? Even though the Dionysian corpus is famous for the so-called *via negationis* as the mode of attaining knowledge of God, we may also discern another path, the *via eminentiae*, to which he most strongly calls us.[17] The best way of describing this path is to say that, whatever we may state about God, at the end of this statement there always remains something hyper,[18] i.e. above and beyond, that which human language can articulate. The end of the path is not negation, but the limits laid out by God's own revelation. Dionysius states that very clearly when he writes that 'one must neither dare to say —nor clearly, to conceive— anything about the hidden divinity beyond being contrary to what has been divinely manifested to us in the sacred writings'.[19] Ultimately, the 'eminence' of God means that He stands 'beyond everything' we can know or speak of Him. This does not discount 'theo-logy'; rather, it keeps it humble.

The fact that God surpasses human reason and rational discourse is something that lies at the beginning of theological contemplation for both the East and the West. Let us not forget that Augustine begins his classic work on the Trinity with a warning against those who 'scorn the starting-point of faith, and allow themselves to be deceived through an unseasonable and misguided love of reason'.[20] Aquinas also lays out at the start of his *Summa* the question concerning the nature of sacred doctrine:

It was necessary for man's salvation that there should be a knowledge revealed by God besides philosophical science built up by human reason. First, indeed, because man is directed to God, as to an end that surpasses the grasp of his reason: 'The eye hath not seen, O God, besides Thee what things Thou has prepared for them that wait for Thee (Isa. 64:4)'.[21]

Finally, as A.N. Williams reminds us, while apophaticism may engender a basic humility, taken as our fundamental approach to God, it ends up depriving us of the joy and gratitude that is borne out of the reception of a gift and the enjoyment of a relationship. Williams writes, 'To say God is unknowable in the face of the divine self-giving that is Scripture is not only to deny what Scripture is —both the record and enactment of divine self-giving— but in that denial, also to fail to receive the gift with joy and thanksgiving.'[22] Scripture is not simply a handbook of knowledge but a gift that, upon our reception of it, draws us into a relationship with its Giver, using the 'words' we have received therein to address our Lover.

(?) Can apophatic theology be reconciled with the way that Scripture describes God?

2

THE PATH TO THE TRUTH:

SCRIPTURE, TRADITION, AND THE CHURCH

'The Bible says…' This phrase became emblematic of the evangelical ethos, largely through the preaching of the world-famous evangelical preacher, Billy Graham. The Bible and what the Bible says is the final argument, the ultimate authority, the end of the discussion. The Bible stands at the centre of the life and faith of the Church, as indicated by the centrality given to the public reading of Scripture and the preaching of the Word in the worship services of any typical evangelical church. Of course, this mindset is inherited from the sixteenth-century Reformation; at the Diet of Worms, Luther said (or,

rather, is alleged to have said) those famous words: 'Here I stand'. Before this, however, he also said the following:

> Unless I am convinced by the testimony of the Scriptures or by clear reason (for I do not trust either in the pope or in councils alone, since it is well known that they have often erred and contradicted themselves), I am bound by the Scriptures I have quoted and my conscience is captive to the Word of God. I cannot and I will not retract anything, since it is neither safe nor right to go against conscience.[23]

This quote helps us identify what in reality is the central issue when we discuss the subject of the relationship between Scripture and Tradition. The chief question concerns what has the final authority over matters of faith and practice. As Protestants, we reply, *sola Scriptura* (the Bible alone). How, though, do the Orthodox reply to the same question? We often make the mistake of assuming that they reply by saying, 'the Bible and Tradition'. In reality, however, their answer is fundamentally, 'the Church'. The title of George Florovsky's book on this subject, *Bible, Church, and Tradition*, is instructive.[24] At the centre of the discussion lies the Church! Let us examine then how!

THE ORTHODOX WAY

In Florovsky's book, we find the following definition:

> Tradition is the witness of the Spirit; the Spirit's unceasing revelation and preaching of good tidings… To accept and

understand Tradition we must live within the Church, we must be conscious of the grace-giving presence of the Lord in it; we must feel the breath of the Holy Ghost in it… Tradition is not only a protective, conservative principle; it is, primarily, the principle of growth and regeneration… Tradition is the constant abiding of the Spirit and not only the memory of words.[25]

This text, I believe, helps us see that for the Orthodox, tradition is not a parallel collection of books or texts, alongside Scripture, but rather a living witness that dwells within the Church. Lossky, furthermore, distinguishes between the Tradition and the traditions, expanding on an idea taken from Basil the Great, who distinguishes between dogma and kerygma. Dogma is the secret teaching that the Church received via the apostles, which remained unarticulated and unspoken. It refers to the fullness of truth, which resides in the Church in a mystical way. This for Lossky is the 'Tradition' that 'is not only kept by the Church—it lives in the Church, it is the life of the Holy Spirit in the Church'.[26]

Whenever, however, it is necessary, the Church articulates various aspects of this Tradition, making what is mystically possessed become publicly expressed. Thus we have the kerygma, or in Lossky's terms, the 'traditions'. Commenting on the distinction between dogma and kerygma in Basil the Great, and following Lossky, Louth writes that the dogmas, '… are not truths that can be proclaimed, they are not "objective" truths which could be appraised and understood outside the bosom of the Church: rather they are part of the Church's reflection on the mystery of her life with God.'[27]

Understood this way, Tradition is 'another way of speaking of the inner life of the Church'[28] or 'an inarticulate living of the mystery' or even 'the tacit dimension'.[29]

The Church thus has a living 'Tradition' and out of this brings forth various 'traditions', which according to Kallistos Ware, are 'the books of the Bible…the Creed… the decrees of the Ecumenical Councils and the writings of the Fathers… the Canons, the Service Books, the Holy Icons—in fact, the whole system of doctrine, Church government, worship, and art which Orthodoxy has articulated over the ages.'[30] In this sense, the discussion is not framed in an adversarial way, as a binary choice: Scripture or Tradition. Rather, Scripture is part of the Tradition which lives within the Church.

AN EVANGELICAL RESPONSE

THE BIBLE AS A BOOK OF THE CHURCH

This emphasis on the Bible as a Book of the Church needs to be a welcomed reminder for Evangelicals.[31] One of the things that evangelical theology has often fallen prey to is a severing of the connection between Scripture and the Church. There are several typical ways that this has taken place. One is an individualistic approach to studying the Bible, whereby each person reads for themselves and understands and interprets according to whatever they think or believe. Even in contexts where the Bible is studied together in groups, one common practice in evangelical circles, is to ask the question, 'What do you think this passage means?' or 'What does it say to you?' receiving the answer, 'I understand this...' or 'It seems to me that this passage says that.'

Another equally problematic instance of the unmooring of the Bible from the Church is when study of Scripture is reduced to an academic exercise. This is seen wherever the Bible is treated simply as a text to be dissected and analysed as part of a scientific process, rather than as a sacred text of the ecclesial community. In response to this, we must return to an emphasis that in order to understand the Scriptures, we need something more than an intellectual or rational investigation; we need the illumination of the Holy Spirit. It is interesting to note that the Bible was not given either to individuals or to universities and libraries. It was given to the Church. What, however, this means needs to be examined and clarified with more precision. Before we do that, though, we need first to underline some other issues with the orthodox understanding of tradition.

DRAWING THE LINE
BETWEEN TRADITION AND TRADITIONS

We begin by noting the difficulty of seeing how this distinction between 'Tradition' and 'traditions' works in real life. Orthodox theologian, Aristotle Papanikolaou, complains that it 'is characteristically vague and formless'.

He writes, 'When contemporary Orthodox theologians assert that tradition is a lived experience, the life of the Holy Spirit, the fullness of the mystery of Christ, there may be some truth to those statements, but one is not sure what that looks like or where to go from there. Beyond simply negating a legalistic understanding of tradition, how do these expressions about tradition help us differentiate between those constitutive elements of the tradition as the experience of the mystery of Christ in the Holy Spirit, and those that are not essential?'[32] The recent controversy in Greece caused by the COVID-19 pandemic regarding the proper means of distributing the Holy Eucharist is a case in point for this ambiguity. Is the use of one spoon part of the Tradition or the traditions? Is it something that the Church knows in a mystical existential fashion or is it something that can be learned by the modern standards of hygiene?[33]

TRADITION AND THE CHURCH: A COMPLEX RELATIONSHIP

Another issue that needs to be clarified is that the relationship between the Church and Tradition is more complicated than it is often assumed. In an unpublished lecture, presented in 2013 in Athens, Andrew Louth[34] brought into focus a dual issue concerning the notion of the Church as the final criterion of truth. The first issue is the fact that many of the patristic texts, which are considered today to be part of the 'truth' of the Church, in reality were not preserved or brought to light by the Church, but actually through scientific and academic research. One salient example is the *Epistle to Diognetus*. Another example would be the fact that the corpus of Maximus the Confessor, accepted today with such enthusiasm amongst orthodox commentators as expressing the riches of the patristic tradition, was rediscovered and made available by western scholars, both catholic and protestant. This raises the question of what we mean when we talk about the 'Church'. To what does this term refer and whom does it include?

The second issue, which takes the form of the reverse of the first, pertains to texts written by authors condemned by the Church as heretics, which nonetheless 'slipped under the net', were preserved in the life of the Church and are now considered to contain 'a wealth of spiritual wisdom and theological reflection'. One such characteristic example are the writings of Evagrius.

ECCLESIOLOGICAL AMBIGUITIES

It is of utmost importance to explain what we refer to when we talk about 'the Church'. Commenting on some popular theological works of recent years produced by Orthodox theologians of the diaspora, Paul Gavrilyuk, rightly notes, 'Orthodox intellectuals could not resist producing an idealized picture of their Church, a "book version" of Orthodoxy.'[35] What exactly are we referring to when we talk about the Church? The question remains: who is the legitimate voice expressing the mind of the Church? How are we to define the 'catholicity' of the

Autocephalous churches are self-governed churches with the right to elect their primates without reference to another Church. In the past the criteria for autochephaly had to do with prestige and history. In modern Orthodox ecclesiological practice the decisive factor is rather nationalism.

Church? One of the most complicated ecclesiological issues today is the relationship of notions of autocephaly, primacy, and conciliarity. And what is the place of the laity, the body of the Church, within this nexus? Based on the recent experience of the ill-fated Panorthodox Synod, all these questions remain open and unresolved.[36]

At the same time, and despite that vagueness, there is complete clarity as to who the true Church is. Gavrilyuk, commenting on Florovsky observes that 'in most cases, Florovsky leaves the referent of the "Church" undefined… He assumes, although he rarely states this assumption explicitly, that the historical referent of the "Church" is continuous with the Greek patristic, Byzantine, and contemporary Eastern Orthodox Church.'[37] Obviously, this exclusionary ecclesiology is a major sticking point for evangelical theology.

TRUTH AND INTUITION

Apart from the ambiguity surrounding definitions of the Church, there is an additional vagueness regarding how Tradition as truth exists and is perceived within the Church. According to the orthodox way, truth is grasped 'intuitively'. In the end, one knows because one knows, and one knows because he or she participates in the Church. Gallaher astutely observes, 'This "vision" of faith in which the truth is received appears to be a sort of indemonstrable intuition, what the Romantics called "intellectual intuition" or "feeling", for we are told that dogma is not a discursive axiom which "is accessible to logical development" but an "intuitive truth."'[38] This intuition is acquired as one participates in and is united with the Church. In other words, the way in which the Church knows is apophatic and mystical. This might be viewed as a form of 'Orthodox taste',[39] which someone either has or does not have; a kind of knowledge of 'knowing before one looks'.[40]

We can see the limits of such an approach by comparing the epistles of Ignatius with the writings of Athanasius the Great. As one reads the epistles of Ignatius, his basic argument seems to be that one remains in the truth by remaining in the Church and under the authority of the bishop. One notable example of this can be found in his *Epistle to the Philadelphians* where his advice on avoiding 'false teaching' is to remain within the Church and not follow the schismatic. His formula of truth is straightforward: 'For all who are of God and Jesus Christ, these are with the bishop'.[41] We encounter the same idea in the *Epistle to the Smyrnaeans*. There, the safe way to avoid being influenced by 'those who hold erroneous opinions' is the simple formula, 'You must all follow the bishop as Jesus Christ (followed) the Father. Let no one do anything apart from the bishop that has to do with the church' (*Epistle to the Smyrnaeans* 6.8.1).[42] The Church, and especially the bishop, is the guarantor of the truth. The Church knows simply because the Church knows. What happens though when the bishops themselves are divided, as with the case of Arius? How does one deal with the question of what is false and what is true, when it is not sufficient to say, 'Whatever your bishop says, he knows'? This is when the need for the Bible as the basis for truth becomes clear, something which emerges even from a cursory reading of Athanasius' *On the Incarnation*.[43] The interpretation of the Bible becomes the focus of the discussion!

There is no 'knowledge' mystically possessed by the Church which is independent from the Scriptures. According to John Behr, the true meaning of the concept of the 'rule of truth' (alternatively, 'rule of faith'), which Irenaeus says resides within the Church, is not a mystical intuitive form of knowledge, but the events of the death and resurrection interpreted 'according to the Scriptures' within the context of a community that proclaims the death of Christ through celebrating the Eucharist.

'The "tradition" appealed to by Irenaeus is not just some customary teaching or practice, but that which the apostles "handed down" as the matrix and the means for encountering the Christ they proclaimed, a particular approach and practice, pivoted upon the Passion of Christ, understood through the Scriptures, and enacted in the Eucharist' in John Behr, *Irenaeus of Lyons: Identifying Christianity* (Christian Theology in Context, Oxford: Oxford University, 2013), 115.

In the same way, we may argue that at the end even for Ignatius it is not the bishop who is the guarantor of truth, but the bishop who affirms the rule of faith, in which the truth resides, something that he makes quite clear at the beginning of his letter.[44]

CHURCH AND SCRIPTURE

Did the Church ever exist without Scripture, or a Bible? Is it correct to say that the Church predated the Bible? The first Christians already had a 'canon', what we now call the Old Testament (Rom. 15:3; 1 Cor. 10:6; 2 Tim. 3:15-16). Moreover the apostolic kerygma and teaching was at the centre of the life of the Church (Acts 2:42) long before the formation and canonisation of the New Testament. Written texts of the apostles, such as the epistles of Paul, were considered Scripture (1 Thess. 2:13; Gal. 1:1-24; 2 Pet. 3:16) from the outset.[45] Consequently, we may say that the Scriptures and the apostolic kerygma are the ground or the seed that gives birth to the Church. At the same time, the moment we refer to 'apostles', we are speaking of people who belong to the Church. It is impossible to distinguish the Church from the Scriptures, and therefore problematic to speak of which comes first and which comes second. Thus, instead of speaking of a Scripture that gives birth to the Church or a Church that gives birth to Scripture, it is preferable to speak of the Holy Spirit who gives birth to both Church and Scripture in a relationship of interdependency.

THE IMPORTANCE OF THE CANON

The dogma of the 'canon of Scripture', which is linked to the question of the Church-Scripture relationship, unfolds quite differently in the context of Protestant theology. Without ever questioning the fact that the 'canon of Scripture' is indeed an ecclesial reality, it is essential to define what exactly we mean by this.

Commenting on Calvin's position, Webster observes that while the Church 'approves' Scripture, this is actually 'a receptive act' rather than an authorisation. It is an act of 'assent' and acknowledgement rather than an adjudication or ruling. Just as the sheep recognise the voice of their Shepherd, the Church recognises the voice of God through a number of holy texts. At the same time, this act has a 'backward reference',[46] as the Church affirms that 'all truthful speech in the Church can proceed only from the prior apostolic testimony'.[47] The Church is apostolic only insofar as it submits to and aligns itself with the Scriptures. In the words of Barth, 'the apostolic succession of the Church must mean that it is guided by the canon'.[48] It is a promise and a commitment to operate according to this 'measure'.

Barth moreover argues:

> With its acknowledgment of the presence of the Canon, the Church expresses the fact that it is not left to itself in its proclamation, that the commission and the ground of which it proclaims, the object which it proclaims, the judgement under which its proclamation stands and the event of real

proclamation must all come from elsewhere, from without, and very concretely from without, in all the externality of the concrete Canon as a categorical imperative which is also historical, which speaks in time.[49]

ECCLESIOLOGICAL IDEALISM
AND THE REALISM OF SOLA SCRIPTURA

It is important to note that the dogma of *sola scriptura* was formulated within an ecclesial experience marked by degeneration and corruption. We might say therefore that this dogma is an emphatic confession that for the Church to remain faithful to her nature, she requires something outside herself, a voice which speaks to her and that she heeds, a standard by which she measures herself and evaluates her health, a foundation that provides her with a 'stability grounded extra ecclesiam'.[50] In other words, despite the many ways it has been used, at the heart of *sola scriptura* lies the basic realisation that the Church is never without sin or compromise. The closed, written canon of Scripture is thus a guarantor, a 'sign' that stands against alteration and distortion. This is the aspect that Barth, rightly, brings to the fore when he insists that the Scriptures as a closed written record needs to be the 'strait gate'[51] which the Church should never bypass. Despite the fact that Scripture may be misinterpreted and wrongly understood, the written and closed nature of the Bible 'guarantees its freedom over against the Church and therefore creates for the Church freedom over against itself.'[52] The virtue of its written nature safeguards for the Church 'the possibility of being recalled by it to the truth, the possibility of the reformation of a Church which has perhaps been led into misunderstanding and error'.[53]

CHURCH, SCRIPTURE, TRADITION, AND THE GOD OF REVELATION

In conclusion, it is important to reframe the whole discussion about truth and revelation within its appropriate 'dogmatic location'.[54] If the horizon of our discussion is purely ecclesiological, then it is extremely limited. The Church neither has existed 'in the beginning', nor exists 'of herself'. The Church exists because the triune God reveals Himself through His Word. As such, the proper horizon of our discussion should be the God who reveals Himself, or more accurately, 'the revelatory self-gift of the triune God which directs the creation to its saving end'.[55]

3

WHAT WENT WRONG?:

THE PROBLEM OF SIN

Towards the end of his treatise, *The Bondage of the Will*, Luther lauds Erasmus for 'unlike the rest, you alone have attacked the real issue, the essence of the matter in dispute…You and you alone have seen the question on which everything hinges…the vital spot'.[56] The question of the human condition after the fall, the diagnosis of the problem, stands at the beginning of the journey of theological reflection concerning salvation. Before we speak of the solution, we must lay out the contours of the problem. At this point we realise that there is a serious problem with the 'problem', as we observe the gulf between the orthodox and the evangelical understanding of the fall, and the resultant human condition. This becomes clear immediately even on the level of terminology. Evangelicals, for instance, speak of 'original sin', whereas the Greek term that Orthodox use is 'ancestral sin' (in Greek, *propatoriko*). This divergence in terminology reflects an essential difference in the theological conception of this matter. Orthodox and Protestant theologians agree that on this subject, there is an unbridgeable divide.

Orthodox theologian, David Bentley Hart, speaks of various elements of 'Augustine's catastrophic misreading of Paul that are so profoundly distasteful to Eastern Christians',[57] offering as one example among others, 'the morbidly forensic understanding of original sin…'[58] For Bentley Hart, such doctrines exemplify differences that are 'quite real, substantial, and irreconcilable'. We hear the same verdict from the opposite side. Protestant theologian, Gerald Bray, concludes his study of 'Original Sin in Patristic Thought' by determining that 'more than perhaps anything else, the doctrine of original sin stands as a monument to two different, and mutually incompatible ways of thinking'.[59] With these absolute statements in mind, we come to this topic. In our approach, we will not follow the path of theological abstraction, but that of narrative. Let us examine then what went wrong, according to the orthodox narrative.

THE ORTHODOX WAY

Theology professor, Stavros Yagazoglou, from the theological faculty of the University of Athens, lays out the basic narrative in his article, 'Sin, freedom, and self-determination', in the Greek Orthodox theological journal, *Synaxis*.[60]

As an image of the cosmos, and as image of God, man has the responsibility and the mission to exercise his free will in order that in time he may commune fully with God, and thus lead the rest of creation into the divine life...

The creation of the world and of humankind was not a completed event, but was and remains dynamically oriented towards an eschatological fullness, since the meaning of the world, and by extension of humanity, is to be found in God himself...man decides to become himself the ultimate centre of reference for the rest of creation...

The initial potential of man to attain likeness with God, in order to unite the whole of creation to the life of the uncreated, was interrupted violently...

The break in the relationship between created and uncreated, brought about by the ancestral sin, can be mended. God's plan remains intact. After all, humankind was already mortal[61] even before death due to its creatureliness...

The original christological prospect now takes a new form...

The self-determination of man, though weakened, still exists and has the potential, as it becomes aware of its straying from the course, to turn and once again move towards God…

This deviation and estrangement of the ancestors from the life of God is inherited by their descendants as a weakness in their human nature, as they partake of the same corrupt nature of the 'garments of skin'…[62]

The solution to the drama and the impasse of created existence within the necessity of corruption and death is provided by God himself…

The solution of Christology to the impasse of the economy of Adam should mean the overcoming of death, not as external and transcendent principle, but within created nature itself as it willingly suffers it…

A new Adam was required.

As we attempt to decipher this narrative, we will focus on several key points.

THE DYNAMISM
OF CREATION AND CREATURELINESS
AS A PROBLEM

The first and most crucial element is that the created order by its very constitution is drawn towards the uncreated, in order to be united to it. As part of this creation, or more precisely 'as priest of creation',[63] man is not created morally perfected but in order to be perfected and through this perfecting to be deified, and through his deification to lead the whole of creation to union with God. Man therefore does not begin from a position of good standing but of deficit. Yagazoglou states elsewhere, 'The salvation of the created being is above all an ontic problem'.[64] As Zizioulas further expounds, in order for man to fulfil his calling as the 'image of God', he must be freed from the necessity and the limitations pertaining to nature and creatureliness.[65]

Another, more typical and much simpler way to note this dynamism is through the well-known distinction made in Orthodox theology between the 'image' and the 'likeness' of God in man. According to Ware's analysis:

> The image, or to use the Greek term the icon, of God signifies our human free will, our reason, our sense of moral responsibility – everything, in short, which marks us out from the animal creation and makes each of us a person. But the image means more than that. It means that we are God's 'offspring' (Acts xvii, 28), His kin; it means that between us and Him there is a point of contact and similarity. The gulf between creature and Creator is not impassable, for because we are in God's image we can know God and have communion with Him. And if we make proper use of this faculty for communion with God, then we will become 'like' God, we will acquire the divine likeness; in the words of John Damascene, we will be 'assimilated to God through virtue'. To acquire the likeness is to be deified, it is to become a 'second god', a 'god by grace'.[66]

DESERTION RATHER THAN FALL

Continuing the above analysis, from the moment that man is 'not yet' but 'called to become', we may not speak of 'fall' in the sense of 'falling from' a certain state. We may only speak of 'failing to' fulfil our calling. It is a form of 'desertion',[67] or abandonment of our mission.

CONSEQUENCE RATHER THAN PUNISHMENT

If then the fall was not the violation of a command but the failure to fulfil a mission, then obviously we cannot make use of legal or forensic terms when speaking of it. The concept of 'guilt' or 'punishment' simply does not make sense here. God is not a magistrate condemning a guilty party, but a Father disappointed by the behaviour of His immature child.

> Adam began in a state of innocence and simplicity. 'He was a child, not yet having his understanding perfected,' wrote Irenaeus. 'It was necessary that he should grow and so come to his perfection.' God set Adam on the right path, but Adam had in front of him a long road to traverse in order to reach his final goal.[68]

As he explains later on, 'Most Orthodox theologians reject the idea of "original guilt", put forward by Augustine and still accepted (albeit in a mitigated form) by the Roman Catholic Church. Humans (Orthodox usually teach) automatically inherit Adam's corruption and mortality, but not his guilt: they are only guilty in so far as by their own free choice they imitate Adam.'[69]

Consider a father who says to his child, 'Don't go outside because it is raining and you will get sick'. A friend of the child comes by and tells him, 'Come and play, everything will be fine'. The child goes out and as a result comes down with pneumonia. Is the pneumonia a punishment from the father or merely the outcome of the child's foolishness? What should the father feel for his child in this circumstance? Wrath or compassion? Anger or love? So, Adam 'is not to be judged too harshly for his error'.[70]

Of course there are consequences since the alienation of man from God, the source of Life, naturally led to the introduction of 'a new form of existence... That of disease and death'.[71] As such, the biggest problem of humanity is not its guilt but its mortality. This is the problem that the loving Father God must help man to overcome, that man may once again have the opportunity to fulfil his mission, to unite the created with the uncreated.

AN EVANGELICAL RESPONSE

THE AFFIRMATION OF THE 'IMAGE OF GOD' IN HUMANITY

Something that needs to be appreciated in the orthodox approach is that it retains the central importance of the image of God in man even after the fall. Evangelical theology is often characterised by a lack of clarity and some confusion regarding this matter. It is often maintained that after the fall, the image of God was lost or at the very least seriously marred.[72] Of course, we must always be careful to define what we mean by the terms we use, especially when it comes to the image of God. If we are to define the image of God as the 'primeval' or 'original righteousness'[73] of man or as moral integrity before God, then we may say that the image has indeed been lost. However, many Evangelicals today are prepared to approach the issue afresh. In this endeavour, an engagement with the orthodox understanding can be beneficial as they are good in emphasising the significance of the image of God in humanity. At the same time, however, we must emphasise that they tend to end up at the other extreme, thereby minimising the effects of the fall. A balanced approach, avoiding either extreme, has been suggested by Michael Horton, who argues that humans in their fallen condition 'have lost not the natural image but the moral ability to fulfil its destiny'.[74]

THE AFFIRMATION
OF THE THEOLOGICAL WEIGHT
OF THE INCARNATION AND THE RESURRECTION

Another positive aspect of the Orthodox narrative lies in the soteriological import given to the events of the incarnation and the resurrection of our Lord. This is a theme that we will return to over the course of the book again and again. The incarnation is often treated by Evangelicals as simply an example of humility and condescension, with the resurrection being approached as a matter for apologetics regarding its historicity. Both of these events, however, have great bearing on the salvific needs of humanity. The union of man with God (via the incarnation), and also the overcoming of the curse of death (via the resurrection), are both part of the salvific intervention and the redemptive economy of God towards man.

FOR GOD 'SO LOVED THE WORLD…'

Finally, and most importantly, the narrative reminds us that the primary motivation for God's movement towards us is His love.

In *Letters and Papers from Prison*, Dietrich Bonhoeffer criticized those styles of evangelistic preaching that seek first to persuade people how wretched and miserable they are and only then introduce Jesus Christ as the cure for their condition. He called it 'religious blackmail'[75] and thought it both ignoble and completely inconsistent with Jesus' own preaching. We have already mentioned Augustine in relation to the doctrine of original sin. As McFarland explains, 'Augustine emphasizes human depravity not for its own sake, out of some sort of *theological misanthropy* (emphasis mine), but as a corollary of the good news of the gospel: that salvation is entirely a matter of grace rather than a product of human effort (Eph. 2:8)'.[76] We must admit that we often speak of the fall almost as if John 3:16 reads, 'for God was *so angry* with the world, that he gave his only begotten Son'. Even though wrath is most certainly part of the narrative (John 3:36), it is important to remember that the heart of the Gospel, contained in this verse, is 'for God *so loved* the world'.

THE PROBLEM OF GUILT, FORENSIC LANGUAGE AND DEATH

The Orthodox understanding of the fall states that 'humans… automatically inherit Adam's corruption and mortality, but not his guilt: they are only guilty in so far as by their own free choice they imitate Adam.'[77] This is why they insist on the term, 'ancestral sin'. The sin was Adam's and Eve's, and it was only the results of this that were transferred to us. It is worth noting that Ware even uses the term 'guilt' here, albeit only referring to the personal sin of the individual, since in general Orthodox theologians avoid forensic language, with some disavowing it altogether.[78]

When we read Romans 5:15–19, however, which speaks of the fall of Adam, we see forensic language being used all over.

> But the free gift is not like the *trespass*. For if many died through one *man's trespass*, much more have the grace of God and the free gift by the grace of that one man Jesus Christ abounded for many. And the free gift is not like the result of that one man's sin. For the judgment following *one trespass brought condemnation*, but the free gift following

many *trespasses brought justification*. For if, because of one man's *trespass*, death reigned through that one man, much more will those who receive the abundance of grace and the free gift of righteousness reign in life through the one man Jesus Christ. Therefore, *as one trespass led to condemnation* for all men, so one act of righteousness leads to *justification* and life for all men. For as by the one *man's disobedience the many were made sinners*, so by the one man's obedience the many will be made righteous...

Here we must pause and explain why we persist in using forensic language. Is it merely an obsession or peculiarity of evangelical theology? The reason we hold on to forensic language, apart from the obvious reason concerning the use of it in Scripture, is because it has broader theological ramifications. If the problem of man is simply death or corruption, then salvation is revivication or healing from corruption. If, however, the problem of man also includes the fact that he is guilty, and therefore liable to punishment, then he also needs to be justified and justification requires a just punishment. That of course has significant ramifications, as we will see in later chapters, in our understanding of the cross and our experience of salvation. Of course, we acknowledge that guilt is not the only result of sin. Sometimes our reaction to the orthodox denial of the notion of guilt leads us to overemphasise it at the expense of other aspects of sin, such as estrangement, degeneration, enslavement, hardness of heart, self-centredness, and even denial of sin.[79]

We believe that the passage from Romans 5, referred to above, shows clearly that death comes as a punishment for a transgression, and not merely as the natural result of a human decision. We see the same thing in Romans 6:23, 'For the wages of sin is death.' Apart, though, from the biblical witness it is common sense and experience that lead us to the same conclusion. As Gerald Bray points out:

> …everyone agrees that Adam died as a result of his sin but that is not the same thing as saying that sin caused him to lose his original immortality. After all, Satan was immortal, but he did not lose that quality when he sinned. On the other hand, the man Jesus Christ was mortal, but that did not prevent him from being sinless as well. The relationship between sin and death therefore seems to be more complex than the Eastern Orthodox church's.[80]

In other words, if death is the natural result and consequence of our departure from God, then why is the devil still alive?

INHERITANCE, RESPONSIBILITY AND CHOICE

We stand before an indisputable fact: in the end all commit sin! Imitating Adam is inevitable! We saw that Orthodox theology insists emphatically that man retains his faculty of self-determination (*autexousion*) even after the fall, so that sin remains a free choice that he makes. At the same time, though, it admits that Adam 'and his descendants passed under the domination of sin and of the devil… Our will is weakened and enfeebled by what the Greeks call "desire" and the Latins "concupiscence". We are all subject to these, "the spiritual effects of original sin"'.[81] In other words, because of Adam and his sin, we will all eventually sin and be found guilty before God. There is therefore no one who freely exercising his power of self-determination ever chooses not to sin.[82] One wonders, therefore, if there is any point in maintaining a notion of self-determination and the distinction between inheritance of guilt on the one hand or corruption that leads inevitably to sin and eventually to guilt on the other since in the end we all sin![83]

REFRAMING THE DOCTRINE OF ORIGINAL SIN

Pressed by our interaction with the Orthodox approach, we need to clarify several aspects of our understanding of original sin. One has to do with the way in which the 'guilt' of Adam's sin becomes ours. This does not entail an impersonal or automatic inheritance. We are not speaking of a mechanistic, unjust, and cold process of imputation and transferal. Due to limitations of space, we may only scratch the surface of this, but suffice to say, evangelical theology at its best supports the idea that we are not guilty 'for' Adam's sin but 'as' sinners 'in Adam'.[84] We are not talking about a blind, collective guilt, but our real participation in 'the presence of the past' of a 'diachronically extended community'.[85]

The second thing to clarify is that when we speak of us being 'sinners' before we have sinned, we do not mean to minimise the fact of our personal responsibility. We maintain the balance between radical responsibility for sin and radical powerlessness in the face of sin. As Moo correctly states, we hold in tension on the one hand the statement of Romans 5:12, 'Each person dies because each person sins' and on the other, that of 5:18a, 'one [man's] trespass resulted in condemnation of all people'.[86]

Finally, we must be careful to locate this discussion within its proper wider theological context. As Behr has shown, Irenaeus claimed that 'the only perspective from which one can contemplate the economy of God, from its beginning to its conclusion, is from the end point, the apocalyptic opening of the Scriptures at the end of the ages in the light of the Cross of Christ'.[87] That is exactly what guides Augustine's understanding of the fall and the human fallen condition. The reason he denies man's faculty of self-determination is purely Christological. As McFarland outlines, 'If the will could overcome sin by its own power, then Christ would have died to no purpose; therefore, it must be the case that the will is able to overcome sin only when empowered by grace.'[88] We note here that God's action is not in competition with human freedom but its essential precondition. The doctrine of original sin thus, as McFarland very poignantly states, is 'a reflex of the gospel'.[89]

We find the same Christological perspective in Athanasius' understanding of the fall in his work *On the Incarnation*.[90] In this work, Athanasius describes God's dilemma after the fall. On the one hand 'He saw that corruption held us all the closer, because it was the penalty for the Transgression' (ch. 8). On the other, He also saw our 'liability to death' and 'pitying our race, moved with compassion for our limitation, unable to endure that death should have the mastery' over us and so 'the work of His Father for us men come to nought' (ch. 8). The cross of Christ is the only solution with the incarnation being the necessary precondition. So 'He took our body' and 'He surrendered His body to death in place of all' (ch. 8) as 'an offering and a sacrifice' (ch. 9) 'in dying a sufficient exchange for all and, [His body] itself remaining incorruptible through His indwelling might thereafter put an end to corruption for all others as well, by the grace of the resurrection' (ch. 9).

I believe that both Augustine and Athanasius, despite their differences, agree that the understanding of the fall and the nature of the problem of sin must always be approached through the lens of Christology and specifically the cross. What must be the nature of our fall and of our sinful condition if the only way to override it, was the death of God's Son on the cross? Even though we stated in the introduction that the question of sin stands at the beginning of theological contemplation, it appears that we must now revisit this statement. Augustine and Athanasius show us a better way arguing that the question 'why was the cross of Christ necessary' is the key that unlocks and illuminates the discussion around the meaning of the fall and the theological reflection on the nature of the problem of sin.

4

THE CROSS OF CHRIST:

CHRISTUS VICTOR AND *AGNUS DEI*

In Christ alone my hope is found;
He is my light, my strength, my song;
…Till on that cross as Jesus died,
The wrath of God was satisfied;
For ev'ry sin on Him was laid—
Here in the death of Christ I live.[91]

Jesus, my great High Priest,
Offered His blood and died;
My guilty conscience seeks no sacrifice beside.
His powerful blood did once atone,
And now it pleads before the Throne.[92]

In both these hymns, one modern and one traditional, we find the basic building blocks which make up the evangelical understanding of the meaning and importance of the cross, namely, 'sacrifice', 'guilt', 'wrath', 'punishment', 'atonement'. How is the cross viewed, however, in the context of Orthodox theology?

THE ORTHODOX WAY

In order to get to the cross and its meaning, we must return to the narrative of redemption which we started unfolding in the previous chapter and pick up the story where we left off. We saw there that for many modern Orthodox theologians, the fall is defined as the failure of humankind to unite the created with the uncreated, and not as violation of a command that renders it guilty before God, and liable to judgement. After the fall, the calling remains the same, with the only difference that it has now become far more difficult to accomplish, due to corruption and mortality. Into this condition comes the salvific intervention of God. Let us see how Yagazoglou describes it:

> The paradoxical intervention of the Son was included in some way already in the positive ascent of the Adamic economy, which entailed a gradual union between the created and the uncreated. Christ is neither the result of sin nor the devil. Where Augustine and Luther focus their teaching on the doctrine of original sin [...] the Greek Fathers insist on viewing the incarnation as the realisation

of the initial purpose of the creation of humanity [...] The incarnation was the absolute and primary goal of God in the act of creation [...] The mystery of the incarnation as the union of created and uncreated in the hypostasis of the Word is constituted by the action and the grace of the Holy Spirit in the Virgin Mary. Divine and human elements both contribute decisively, in their own respective ways, in its realisation, so that the truth of the incarnation depends on the integrity and fullness in Christ of both divinity and humanity.[93]

As one may easily discern, the basic soteriological event in the Orthodox narrative of redemption is the incarnation, given that salvation is defined as the union of the created with the uncreated, of man with God. That which the first Adam failed to accomplish, the second Adam will now fulfil. The incarnation is precisely this perfect union for which humankind was created in the first place. The fall, however, made the incarnation 'not only an act of love but an act of salvation'.[94]

Similarly Lossky writes:

'God made Himself man, that man might become God.' These powerful words, which we find for the first time in St. Irenaeus, are again found in the writings of St. Athanasius, St. Gregory of Nazianzus, and St. Gregory of Nyssa. The Fathers and Orthodox theologians have repeated them in every century with the same emphasis, wishing to sum up in this striking sentence the very essence of Christianity: an ineffable descent of God to the ultimate limit of our fallen human condition, even unto death — a descent of God which opens to men a path of ascent, the unlimited vistas of the union of created beings with the Divinity. The descent (κατάβασις) of the divine person of Christ makes human persons capable of an ascent (ἀνάβασις) in the Holy Spirit.[95]

Later, he continues:

It was necessary that the voluntary humiliation, the redemptive κένωσις, of the Son of God should take place, so that fallen men might accomplish their vocation of θέωσις, the deification of created beings by uncreated grace. Thus the redeeming work of Christ—or rather, more generally speaking, the Incarnation of the Word is seen to be directly related to the ultimate goal of creatures: to know union with God.[96]

All these are summarised poignantly by Florovsky when he writes that, 'the whole history of christological dogma was determined by this basic idea: the Incarnation of the Word, as Salvation'.[97] It is clear, then, that for many Orthodox the incarnation seems to be an event of primary importance for our salvation. The question then is why the cross was necessary. As we have already seen, our soteriological orientation towards union with God has been impaired by death, which is the fundamental consequence of the fall and our subsequent enslavement by the devil. Death, therefore, must be defeated, releasing us from the power by which the devil and sin rule over us. God does that through the cross as the well-known Orthodox hymn of the Easter liturgy proclaims: 'Christ has been raised from the death, having defeated death by death'. Of interest here is that the meaning of the cross is being interpreted by a hymn of the Resurrection. Despite the apparent weakness and frailty, it is *Christus Victor*[98] who is nailed to the cross in order to liberate humans from the tyranny of the Devil 'granting life to those in the tombs'.[99] Lossky comments:

> The Son of God came down from heaven to accomplish the work of our salvation, to liberate us from the captivity of the devil, to destroy the dominion of sin in our nature, and to undo death, which is the wages of sin. The Passion, Death, and Resurrection of Christ, by which His redemptive work was accomplished, thus occupy a central place in the divine dispensation for the fallen world.[100]

And further down, correlating the incarnation with the cross, he writes:

> Since the first Adam missed his vocation of free attainment of union with God, the Second Adam, the divine Word, accomplished this union of the two natures in His Person, when He was incarnate. Entering the actuality of the fallen world, He broke the power of sin in our nature, and by His death, which reveals the supreme degree of His entrance into our fallen state, He triumphed over death and corruption.[101]

We might summarise, therefore, the Orthodox understanding on the cross, using Ware's phrase, 'the Cross is an emblem of victory'.[102]

AN EVANGELICAL RESPONSE

THE 'WHAT' AND 'WHO' OF THE CROSS

There are various aspects of the orthodox approach that we would do well to take on board as Evangelicals. It is first of all a helpful reminder to arrive at the cross starting from the incarnation. The orthodox emphasis on the incarnation exposes a deficiency in the protestant approach. Of course, a recovery of the significance of the incarnation and its connection to the cross does not necessarily need to follow the same path as that of Orthodox theology. I would like to propose two potentially fruitful ways.

The first is to determine the meaning of the cross by focussing not only on the 'what' but also the 'who'. Our focus is often exclusively on 'what' took place on the cross. As the incarnation comes more into view, however, it becomes clear that an equally important question is 'who is the one who dies on the cross'. This is brought out especially by the analysis of Athanasius in his work, *On the Incarnation*. He begins discussing 'what' happens on the cross, but then he turns his attention to the 'who'. The first dilemma he notes concerning the salvation of the sinner pertains to how God can uphold His law, and judge humankind, while still showing His loving-kindness towards His creatures by saving them. The answer is the 'death' of God. This gives rise to the second dilemma. How is it possible for the immortal to die, and for the impassible to suffer? The incarnation is the answer. Thus, the cross has salvific power precisely because the one who is lifted up there is both perfect man and perfect God.

A second way for the retrieval of the significance of the doctrine of the incarnation is to consider the cross as the result, rather than the cause, of God's decree 'to become one with us as saviour'. By beginning the history of redemption with the incarnation, in other words by giving soteriological import to the incarnation, we confess that it was not the work of the cross that necessitated God's action to save us; rather, it was God's prior decision to be 'Emmanuel', God with us, that necessitated the cross.[103]

CHRISTUS VICTOR AND AGNUS DEI

A second useful aspect that emerges from our dialogue with the orthodox position is the recovery of the importance of the idea of victory and triumph signified by the cross. A growing number of evangelical theologians today are now incorporating this aspect in their treatments of the cross.[104] The witness of the Scriptures to this fuller and broader understanding of the cross is indisputable. For example, we read in Colossians 2:13-15:

> And you, who were dead in your trespasses and the uncircumcision of your flesh, God made alive together with him, having forgiven us all our trespasses, by canceling the record of debt that stood against us with its legal demands. This he set aside, nailing it to the cross. He disarmed the

> rulers and authorities and put them to open shame, by triumphing over them in him.

Also in Colossians 1:13-14:

> He has delivered us from the domain of darkness and transferred us to the kingdom of his beloved Son, in whom we have redemption, the forgiveness of sins.

One particularly noteworthy passage is Hebrews 2:14–17:[105]

> Since therefore the children share in flesh and blood, he himself likewise partook of the same things, that through death he might destroy the one who has the power of death, that is, the devil, and deliver all those who through fear of death were subject to lifelong slavery. For surely it is not angels that he helps, but he helps the offspring of Abraham. Therefore he had to be made like his brothers in every respect, so that he might become a merciful and faithful high priest in the service of God, to make propitiation for the sins of the people.

In all of these texts, the understanding of the cross as both 'victory' and 'sacrifice' stand side by side. The salvific work of Christ thus acquires a greater depth, while taking on new dimensions. As underlined by Rutledge, the aspect of victory 'over the alien Powers of Sin and Death' is connected with the concept of the Kingdom of God and is strongly oriented to the future.[106] Christ's work on the cross is not just for the individual and in view of the past, but concerns the restoration of the whole of creation and it is future oriented. This can be summarised neatly with the memorable phrase of Gregory of Nazianzus, 'Nothing can be compared with the miracle of my salvation: a few drops of blood remake the whole universe'.[107]

Our disagreement therefore with the orthodox approach is not with what it affirms but with what it rejects. Hart's complaint about Lossky's treatment of Western approaches to atonement is telling: 'One enters entirely into the atmosphere of the Orthodox suspicion of Anselm (and by extension, of all Western theology) in Vladimir Lossky's altogether damning portrait of his theory of atonement.'[108] What we take issue with here is the absolute rejection or at best the marginalisation of the notion of penal substitution and propitiation as additional ways to understand the cross. We will now proceed to examine these two ideas to see whether they are true and useful and therefore necessary for our understanding of the work of Christ on the cross.

DEFENDING PENAL SUBSTITUTION

Before we examine the biblical witness to penal substitution, it would be helpful to lay out a definition of what we mean by this term. Letham defines it thus: 'Christ himself willingly submitted to the just penalty which we deserved, receiving it on our behalf and in our place so that we will not have to bear it ourselves'.[109] Simon Gathercole has a similar definition, 'When Christ died bearing our sins or guilt or punishment, he did so in our place and instead of us'.[110] Gathercole references a series of passages that in his opinion support the above definition. Characteristic of these is the use of Isaiah 53:12 in Romans 4:25 and Isaiah 53:6 in Romans 8:32. He also notes the use of the term ὑπέρ (hyper) in 1 Corinthians 15:3-4 and Romans 5:6-8.[III] The statement that stands as perhaps the most clear witness to the idea of substitution—not only with the sense of 'in our place' but also 'instead of us'— ironically comes from the mouth of Caiaphas, the Jewish high priest. We read in John 11:49-52:

> But one of them, Caiaphas, who was high priest that year, said to them, 'You know nothing at all. Nor do you understand that it is better for you that one man should die for the people, not that the whole nation should perish.' He did not say this of his own accord, but being high priest that year he prophesied that Jesus would die for the nation, and not for the nation only, but also to gather into one the children of God who are scattered abroad.

Apart from the idea of 'substitution', we must also address the notion of punishment, since we are talking about penal substitution. We have already seen how the Orthodox understanding of the fall has no place for the idea of guilt. As a result any idea of the cross as 'punishment' will naturally be viewed by them as strange or problematic. It is important therefore to explain why we insist on viewing the cross in this way. To answer this question, it is worth examining why Christ had to die in the way He did, on the cross. Would it have been sufficient for Him to die in any other way? This question is posed in a pertinent way by Athanasius in his *On the Incarnation*. Would the death of Christ have the same meaning if He died of sickness or of natural causes? Does the choice to go specifically to the cross have any particular significance? As Fleming Rutledge notes, 'Churches sometimes offer Christian education classes under the title "Why did Jesus have to die?" This is not really the right question. A better one is "Why was Jesus crucified?" The emphasis needs to be, not just on the death, but on the manner of death.'[112] Calvin, in his *Institutes*, explains:

> The form of Christ's death also embodies a singular mystery. The cross was accursed, not only in human opinion but by decree of God's law [Deut. 21:23]. Hence, when Christ is hanged upon the cross, he makes himself subject to the curse. It had to happen in this way in order that the whole curse—which on account of our sins awaited us, or rather lay upon us—might be lifted from us, while it was transferred to him... The cross, to which he was nailed, was a symbol of this, as the apostle testifies: 'Christ redeemed us from the curse of the law, when he became a curse for us. For it is written, "Cursed be every one who hangs on a tree," that in Christ the blessing of Abraham might come upon the Gentiles' [Gal. 3:13-14; Deut. 21:23].[113]

The kind of death that Christ died points directly to the idea of 'penalty' and 'punishment'. Giorgio Agamben, in presenting Dante's appraisal of the connection between the cross and punishment, comments that, 'Christ's crucifixion is not a simple "penalty," but a "legitimate punishment (*punitio*)," inflicted by an ordinary judge who, as representative of Caesar, had jurisdiction over the entire human race, which could be ransomed from sin only in this way'.[114]

Is the association of the cross with punishment and penalty, however, a repulsive or unintelligible idea and for this reason unnecessary in our day and age? Rutledge commenting on the fact that 'in recent years, numerous voices have been raised against the idea of a "punitive" interpretation of the cross' argues that 'if we accept the idea that some things "cannot go unpunished" do we not have to entertain the possibility that the event on Golgotha has something to do with God's ultimate sentence upon all the evils in the world?'[115] We shall, however, return to this later.

THE CROSS AS 'ATONEMENT'

A few years ago, I was talking with a well-known Orthodox Greek theologian, when he said to me, 'What is it with your God, that he gets so offended that he can't work things out with himself…?' The theologian would be correct if the notion of offence was associated with God's honour, understood with the sense of egotism and pride. St. Athanasius, however, explained that God's honour is connected primarily with His goodness which is then explained and understood as His consistency and faithfulness. According to David Bentley-Hart's astute analysis, Athanasius in his work *On the Incarnation*:

Lamenting the loss of humanity's original beauty in the fall, argues that redemption was necessitated by God's agathotes (consistency, righteousness, honor, glory), which requires the maintenance and execution of his twin decrees that, on the one hand, humanity will share in the divine life and that, on the other, death must fall upon the transgressors of holy law; to prevent the second decree from defeating the first, guilt must be removed from humanity through the exhaustion of the power of death in Christ's sacrifice.[116]

God's honour then has nothing to do with the idea of a wounded pride or bruised ego but with His commitment to execute faithfully His decrees.

Another concept that requires further clarification is that of God's 'righteousness'. As has been forcefully argued by Miroslav Volf in his book *Free of Charge*, when we speak of the need for satisfaction of divine righteouness, we are not referring to a pre-Socratic notion of some kind of transcendent and autonomous righteousness, outside and above God Himself. In reality, the moral law and righteousness itself are neither above nor outside of God, but are an expression of the divine being.[117] They flow out of and are consistent with Himself.

Finally, when we come to the idea of atonement, we also need to explain the concept of God's wrath. Fleming Rutledge has developed an especially helpful explanation of the significance of this concept, touching also upon the ramifications of assessing it in a certain way. She first clarifies that the wrath of God 'is not an emotion that flares up from time to time as though God had temper tantrums; it is a way of describing his absolute enmity against all wrong and his going to set matters right'.[118] She notes that all of us know deep down that there are some things 'that cannot go unpunished'. As Volf also maintains, 'non-indignant God would be an accomplice in injustice, deception, and violence'.[119] In other words, what should seem appalling and wrong to us must be impunity and not wrath and justice. In fact and in our day, Rutledge observes, 'In our haste to flee from the wrath of God, we might ask whether we have thought through the consequences of belief in a god who is not set against evil in all its forms.'[120] If in the place of outrage before evil we prefer a God who simply forgives and forgets, then our faith and our gospel appear to ignore that fact that 'in our world, something is terribly wrong and must be put right'.[121] If God's way were to bring about an easy 'closure' to the problem of evil and sin, if He followed the advice of 'moving on' and 'putting it behind you', then He would be complicit in the full legitimisation of evil, abuse and violence. It is therefore necessary, both biblically and apologetically, to hold onto the notion of wrath within the nexus of elements that pertain to the work of Christ. It is not the central idea, but

'The wrath of God was satisfied'? This phrase draws from the satisfaction theory of atonement formulated by Anselm of Canterbury (1033 - 1109) who explained Christ's death as the satisfaction paid to God's offended dignity. Here, however, one must be careful. As Michael Horton explains, 'While Anselm grounds the atonement in the need to satisfy God's offended dignity, Reformation theology recognised that it was God's justice that was at stake' (Horton, *The Christian Faith*, 504).

it is an inescapable one. For the biblical witness, love and wrath are not mutually-exclusive but coexist side by side as opposite sides of the same coin. Thus, Revelation speaks of the Lamb who is 'slain' (chapters 4-5) but also about the 'wrath of the Lamb' (6:16). John's Gospel similarly speaks of how much God 'loved the world' (3:16) but then, almost in the same breath, of 'the wrath of God' which 'remains on them' (3:36).

REFRAMING ATONEMENT

Having explained why penal substitution and atonement on the one hand, alongside the idea of the victory over death, the devil and sin on the other, are together the two pillars essential for a correct understanding of the cross, it is worth turning now to how the orthodox understanding of the cross helps us to reframe more correctly the idea of the cross as sacrifice and atonement.

The Cross and the Trinity

First of all, we need to relocate the cross within the operations of the Trinity. Two of the most popular examples used by Evangelicals to describe the nature of the sacrifice on the cross are that of the 'railway' and the 'courtroom'. In the first example, the station manager switches the points to rescue the clueless passengers on a passing train, killing his wandering son who has no idea what is going on and should not have been standing around on a railway track in the first place.[122] In the other example, after the condemnation of the guilty party by the magistrate of the court, the defence attorney bargains with the magistrate, offering to suffer the penalty of the condemned in his place. The problem with both of these examples is that they present to us a divided Trinity, or alternatively, they fail to locate the cross 'among the inseparable operations of the Trinity'.[123] We must be especially careful while speaking of the atonement to ensure that we are not giving the impression that on the cross the Father 'is doing' something to the Son or that the Son 'is doing' something to the Father. John Stott outlines this clearly, 'We must never make Christ the object of God's punishment or God the object of Christ's persuasion, for both God and Christ were subjects not objects, taking the initiative together to save sinners'.[124] As the Apostle Paul writes, 'in Christ God was reconciling the world to himself' (2 Cor 5:19, in Greek it's emphatic, 'God, was in Christ…'). He does not say, as Volf notes, 'Christ was reconciling an angry God to a sinful world' nor that 'Christ was reconciling a sinful world to a loving God. Rather: God in Christ was "reconciling the world to himself"'.[125]

Disenchanting sacrifice

The work of Christ does not bring about a 'change' in God's disposition. In the pagan understanding, such as in the example of Iphigenia of the Greek tragedy, 'sacrifice' was a means of appeasing the gods. The logic of sacrifice is that someone does something that results in a change of disposition in someone else. In the case of God, however, as we have just noted in the context of the inseparable operations of the Trinity, God is always the subject in the work of salvation and never the object. In a comprehensive study of the verb, 'καταλλάσσω-ἀποκαταλλάσσω' (reconcile), Stanley Porter[126] shows how in the epistles of Paul, this word takes on a unique sense. In all of ancient literature, the one who is the subject seeking reconciliation is always the offending party. There is only one reference to a third party who works to reconcile two others. In 2 Corinthians 5, we have the first instance of the offended party taking the initiative and functioning in an active sense (also in Rom. 5:8-11, Col. 1:20, and Eph. 2:16). The work of Christ is not a 'means' or 'cause' to change the disposition of God, but the 'result' of God's saving decision to reconcile the world to Himself. Because God loved the world, He gave His Son. It is not the offer of Christ that causes Him to love the sinner but the reverse. As we saw also in the previous chapter, we must not allow our message to reverse the sense of John 3:16, as if it read, 'for God was so wrathful with the world....' Our message must be clear, that it was 'for God so loved the world...'!

WHY PENAL SUBSTITUTION REMAINS NECESSARY

It Gives Us Assurance in the Present

We have already made reference to Rutledge's observation that the understanding of the cross as victory 'over the alien Powers of Sin and Death' is linked to the idea of the kingdom of God and has a strong future orientation. If the cross is only 'victory' then we may only experience its benefits in the present partially and in a limited form. Sin and death continue to be a fact of life and their power still affects us. The 'it is finished', proclaimed from Jesus' lips on the cross, can only give us hope for the future, without anything tangible and final in the present. When we take into account, however, the atonement and penal substitution, we receive assurance in the present too. God has forgiven us, accepted us, and justified us, and this is a final and definitive reality. The cross is the place where I meet the God of love and where He makes me His own through the sacrifice of His Son.

The Problem of Theodicy

Another important feature that brings out the significance of the cross as something more than simply a 'victory' is the subject of theodicy. Operating within the confines of this one-sided horizon of the Orthodox understanding of the cross as simply and only 'victory' over death, David Bentley Hart, in his book *The Doors of the Sea*,[127] sees the resurrection as the only answer provided in the face of the problem of suffering and death. God will one day decisively and finally defeat and overturn evil. This, however, can very easily lead to a 'theology of glory' or 'of the obvious'. Of course we can all see the God of Easter Sunday. Is God, however, lovingly and actively present also on Good Friday? Can pain become an instrument in the fulfilment of God's plans? Can all things work together for the good within the providence and sovereignty of God?[128] I believe that the preservation of the penal substitutionary aspect of the atonement is the key to engage with these agonising and eminently practical questions before all of us.

5

THE 'TELOS' OF SALVATION:

THE DOCTRINE OF DEIFICATION

'If someone asks "How can I become god?" the answer is very simple'.[129] This statement, completely natural for the prominent orthodox theologian, Metropolitan Kallistos Ware, causes the Evangelical to feel quite uneasy. As Ware notes, however, 'Basil described the human person as a creature who has received the order to become a god'. And he continues, saying that, 'such according to the teaching of the Orthodox Church, is the final goal at which every Christian must aim: to become god, to attain *theosis*, "deification" or "divinization".'[130] What do we mean, though, when we speak of deification?

THE ORTHODOX WAY

One of the most critical concerns addressing this subject is to define precisely, insofar as this is possible, the term, 'deification'. In his classic work on deification, Norman Russell attempts to outline and classify the various ways in which this term has been used.[131] We will summarise the main ones below.

For some, deification, is conceived of as attaining 'moral perfection'. Through moral purification and the ascetic striving towards virtue, the believer begins to resemble God more and more, and is thus deified. The key term to grasp here is 'mimesis'. The path to deification and its basic content is the imitation of God.

For others, deification entails a kind of ontological transformation. Through the incarnation of Christ, human nature was united with the divine nature. Through this union, human nature was deified, subjected to a 'good alteration' (καλή ἀλλοίωση).[132] According to a popular formulation by Christos Yannaras, in the experience of deification, 'The created exists in the mode of being of the uncreated'. The key to understand this experience is participation, or more accurately, the realism of the participation of man in God. As man participates really in Christ, and is united with Him, he acquires the ontological ground for union between the created and the uncreated, namely, for deification. This union takes place through the sacraments of the Church and principally through baptism and the Eucharist.

Finally, there is a third understanding of deification, which we shall call the hesychastic approach. This describes a mystical experience, during which the faithful, after a period of *hesychia* (stillness) and prayer, contemplates God as uncreated light and through the reception of this uncreated, divine energy, finds his existence to be deified, so that he may no longer be subject to his natural limitations as he participates in the divine life. This definition is associated with the ascetic tradition and experience. As Russell notes, this final approach became especially popular, both in Greece and in general, chiefly through the work of a group of prominent mid-20th Century theologians, such as Vladimir Lossky and John Meyendorff.

Georgios Mantzaridis describes it:

The theme of uncreated light lies at the heart of Palamas' teaching on the deification of man; it also formed the central point in what is known as the 'hesychastic dispute' during the fourteenth century in Thessaloniki.... The hesychast monks of Mount Athos, in practicing pure prayer, progressed toward the vision of divine light. This light was not considered to be a created symbol of the divine glory but the uncreated grace and energy of God. As the sun lights the world by means of its natural brilliance, so God, by means of His natural energy and grace, illuminates men.... The hesychast monks of Mount Athos, in receiving the radiance of uncreated light, were experiencing direct communion with God, together with all the regenerative and deifying consequences of this. Uncreated light, according to the teaching of Palamas and of the hesychasts in general, is the divining gift of the Holy Spirit, 'this glory of the divine nature, whereby God has communion with the saints.' This light is not only visible to man but is participable by him, and participating in it he is deified.[133]

The above classification has been generalised and simplified somewhat, but I hope that it helps us to understand at least the importance of explaining more precisely what we mean when we refer to deification.

AN EVANGELICAL RESPONSE

DEIFICATION IN OTHER WORDS?

Is deification a completely alien concept to Evangelical theology or is it something that we hold to also but refer to by using different words? Are we, to put it differently, talking about the same thing using different terminology?

One might argue that by defining deification as moral perfection we are really talking about what Evangelicals refer to as sanctification. In Philippians 2:13 we hear Paul saying to the Philippians that God 'works in you, both to will and to work for his good pleasure'. We see therefore that God works (*energei*) in us, moving us to will and to work (*energein*) according to 'his good pleasure'. One of the key theological presuppositions underlying the doctrine of deification is the distinction between the 'essence' and the 'energies' of God. First of all comes the uncreated essence of God which is unapproachable. Then comes created reality. In addition to the created world and the uncreated essence of God, the Orthodox also speak of the 'uncreated energies' of God. Just as the rays of the sun are 'sun' without their being 'the sun', so the energies of God are uncreated, and as such denote the actual and real presence of God. We might say, therefore, that it is the 'uncreated energies' of God that are at work within us, transforming us into the likeness of God. In order, however, to avoid the danger of the energies of God being perceived as an impersonal entity or as a division within God Himself, it would be more accurate and consistent with the language of the New Testament to speak of the Holy Spirit as a person who 'works' in the life of the Church and the believer.

We might also speak of deification, referring to the realism of participation of the believer through Christ in the life of the triune God, as equivalent to the experience we refer to as 'union with Christ'. This experience was of central importance to Calvin[134] and to a degree also in the approach of Luther.[135] Remaining in the Epistle to the Philippians, we read the following in chapter 3:8-10:

> Indeed, I count everything as loss because of the surpassing worth of knowing Christ Jesus my Lord. For his sake I have suffered the loss of all things and count them as rubbish, in order that I may gain Christ and be found in him, not having a righteousness of my own that comes from the law, but that which comes through faith in Christ, the righteousness from God that depends on faith— that I may know him and the power of his resurrection, and may share his sufferings, becoming like him in his death.

Here, the apostle Paul speaks of a real union with Christ, of participation not only of Christ in us but also of us in Him. The question, to which we shall return later, is how this participation takes place and what exactly it means. However and for now if deification is taken merely to indicate a real participation of the believer 'in Christ', or as Panagiotis Nellas puts it, 'life in Christ',[136] I do not believe that any Evangelical would or should have any serious problem accepting it.[137]

Finally, when speaking of deification as ontological transformation,[138] we could view this as equivalent to the glorified state spoken of by Paul in Romans 8:30, where he writes, 'And those whom he predestined he also called, and those whom he called he also justified, and those whom he justified he also glorified'. Of course, we cannot describe this state of the glorification of human existence with any kind of accuracy. What we need to emphasise here is that man does not become 'something more than human, but he does become more human'.[139] As Bonhoeffer says, 'God becomes man and we have to recognise that God wishes us men, too, to be real men.'[140] To state it more explicitly, 'God became man so that man will become man'! An especially useful definition of deification which in effect states this very thing comes to us from Andrew Louth, who clarifies that 'here is perhaps a good place to clear up a misconception about deification, namely, that it involves the transformation of our human nature into something other than human, some kind of apotheosis that removes our humanity'. He further states that, 'the aim of the Christian is to become once again truly human, to become human partners of God as we were originally created, and as human partners to share in the divine life'.[141]

A series of passages (Rom. 8:18-25, 1 Cor. 13:12, 15:45, 2 Cor. 3:18, 1 John 3:2) and also images-events (i.e. the transfiguration of the Lord in Matthew 17:2, the shining face of Moses in Exodus 34:29, the experience of Stephen in Acts 7:55-56) speak to us of an experience of transformation of our fallen humanity. One further reference from Philippians 3:20-21 reads, 'But our citizenship is in heaven, and from it we await a Saviour, the Lord Jesus Christ, who will transform our lowly body to be like his glorious body, by the power that enables him even to subject all things to himself'. Here we see the promise that the 'power' (*energeia*) of God will transform our bodies to be like the glorious body of our risen Lord. Despite being a future experience, we might say that this glory is already being manifested in our lives. I remember a while back an Iranian pastor telling me about his visits to a refugee camp. He was explaining how he would find believers there and disciple them. When I asked him how he was able to pick out those believers amongst a sea of unknown people, he replied, 'From their face'.

The hesychastic version of deification, especially when associated with the experience of the vision of uncreated light, is the one that seems most problematic for Evangelical theology. We encounter it primarily in the work of Gregory Palamas, brought to prominence and popularity in more recent times, mainly by Lossky.[142]

Alongside Palamas, another figure equally important for Lossky's analysis is Dionysus the Areopagite. It is worth looking at a portion from the beginning of the first chapter of Dionysus' work *Mystical Theology*:

> I counsel that, in the earnest exercise of mystic contemplation, thou leave the senses and the activities of the intellect and all things that the senses or the intellect can perceive, and all things in this world of nothingness, or in that world of being and that, thine understanding being laid to rest, thou strain (so far as thou mayest) towards an union with Him whom neither being nor understanding can contain.[143]

According to the Areopagite, in order to attain deification, one must engage in ascetic striving with a view to reaching a state of *apathy*.[144] This state is achieved through various hesychastic practices, above all through the continual repetition of the Jesus Prayer. This striving 'raises man from earth to heaven and, surpassing every celestial name, eminence and dignity, it presents him to God who is above all things.'[145] Note here the importance of the idea of the 'ascent' of man to God. Through this ascetic striving, the hesychast reaches a vision of the uncreated light, which, though not the essence of God itself, is nevertheless uncreated divine energy, and therefore constitutes true participation in God. This experience is akin to that of the disciples on Mount Tabor, during which they went through a transfiguration which allowed them to see the uncreated light with their natural eyes. Through this vision and the participation in it, man is deified.

As we have already noted, this is the version of deification that evokes the most scepticism from Evangelicals, for various reasons. One fundamental stumbling block for Evangelicals is that this view stands on very shaky ground biblically. In considering the experience of the disciples on Tabor, it is important to emphasise that the disciples do not see an impersonal light but persons in the context of the economy of redemption; they see the face of our Lord, but also that of Elijah and Moses. The vision is also explained to them through a clear word from heaven.

The experience of the apostle Paul on the road to Damascus, despite being used frequently as an analogue to hesychastic deification, is not equivalent at all. First of all, it describes a conversion experience that Paul was not seeking. It was not the crowning achievement of a process of purification and prayer. On the contrary, it was a traumatic experience rather than a therapeutic one. Saul's blinding was painful, not comforting. Finally, it was accompanied by a 'word', as God spoke to Paul audibly. As Jordan Cooper has argued, despite Lossky's protestations, 'The Dionysian approach to theotic experience mirrors that of neoplatonic philosophy in many ways' (Cooper, *Christification*, 11-18).

Another problematic feature of this view is the association of this experience of meeting God with a 'technique', such as the repetition of the Jesus Prayer, with the attendant mandated bodily stance and system of breathing.[146] Lossky writes:

The mystical experience which is inseparable from the way towards union can only be gained in prayer and by prayer…

prayer must become perpetual, as uninterrupted as breathing or the beating of the heart. For this a special mastery is needed, a technique of prayer which is a complete spiritual science, and to which monks are entirely dedicated.[147]

We can very easily see how this understanding gives rise to a division within the Church between the 'deified few' and the rest, as the pursuit of such an experience requires one to become a monk or a nun in order to accomplish it. This has even become a point of contention within the Orthodox Church itself as there is disagreement between those who emphasise the eucharistic experience of church life and those who focus on the mysticism of the ascetic life.[148] Apart, though, from such internal disagreements, the idea that the experience of deification is attained through the mystical life by ascetic striving and hesychia is an impossible task for a person living a normal everyday life. I remember Norman Russell giving a lecture a few years ago in Athens, with the title 'Why does Theosis fascinate Western Christians?'[149] At the end of his talk, a well-known Orthodox bishop posed the following pertinent question: 'If redemption is deification, and this requires ascesis and prayer, how can I help my parishioners in their daily struggle with work, family and obligations, to live it out?' I do not remember if any answer was given... Neither am I satisfied with the position of Kallistos Ware, who, faced with this ideal of deification, suggests that, 'every true Christian tries to love God and to fulfil his commandments; and so long as we sincerely seek to do that, then however weak our attempts may be and however often we may fall, we are already in some degree deified.'[150] This comes across as simply a call for us to 'do the best we can and everything will be alright in the end.'

LOCATING DEIFICATION

For many the use of the terminology of deification is a way of bridging the divide between the various Christian traditions.[151] These conversations, however, are often characterised by ambiguity. As we have already noted, there is more than one way in which deification is construed within Orthodox circles. It is crucial, therefore, in such discussions to define clearly what we mean by this term. Moreover, apart from this, there is another distinction to be made. This distinction is often made by Orthodox theologians when commenting on the use of the term, 'deification', by evangelical, and more broadly protestant theologians. Andrew Louth argues that deification has a 'place' in orthodox theology. It thus only makes sense 'in the whole Orthodox experience, including the pattern of theology'. It is located within a broader theological 'mosaic' that spans the doctrines of incarnation, cosmology, eschatology, anthropology, ecclesiology, and soteriology, and it is there that the doctrine acquires its specific meaning and content.[152]

Following on from this observation, Paul Gavrilyuk distinguishes between a 'broad definition' and a 'more developed understanding'.[153] For Gavrilyuk, to speak of deification as a dogma, it is essential to understand it as existing within a theological context, that for him includes a synergistic anthropology, sacramental realism and the distinction between the essence and energies of God. I would add here also the metaphysical paradigm that grounds this whole project.

We shall thus proceed to examine each of the above topics.

Deification and Its Metaphysical Paradigm

Often, the most important issues are hidden at the unseen level of presuppositions. This proves to be the case here, as one of the most critical points regarding deification and its reception amongst Evangelicals is the matter of the metaphysical paradigm in which it is approached. I remember a conversation from a few years back with an acquaintance of mine who, at the time, was quite attracted to Orthodox theology. He took a napkin and drew two circles, with the larger one on top and the smaller one underneath it. The larger circle, he said is God, and the smaller one is creation, the world, humanity. This is your view of reality, he said to me. Then, next to this first diagram, he drew a new one. In this one there was a large circle, and within this large circle were those same two circles from the first diagram, one large one above, and one smaller one below. This is the Orthodox view, he said. This description may very well be an oversimplification, but I believe that it brings out a key issue that colours, affects, and even determines our discussion regarding deification.

What is the relationship of God with creation in general and with humanity in particular? According to Hallonsten, in the East, 'Creation from its very beginning is seen as a participation in God.'[154] Thus, there is an unbreakable bond between nature and grace, and according to the Platonic conception of reality, grace 'inheres in it and potentially leads it to union with God'. Dumitru Staniloae writes characteristically:

> God is an endless source of spiritual energy open to the world and the world is capable of being open in its own innermost depths to this energy...the world is open to God and God is open to the world, but each preserves its own freedom....there are channels through which God communicates his energy to the world. For example, God, as a matter of course, communicates to the world the energy required to keep in existence, but it is only if the world, through the mediation of man, actively desires it, that God communicates to it his transfiguring energy.[155]

Similarly, A. N. Williams, in the context of her comparative study of Palamas and Aquinas on the issue of deification, supports the idea that the 'infallible marker of the doctrine, is the union of God and humanity, when this union is conceived as humanity's incorporation into God, rather than God's into humanity'.[156] This reference to 'human participation in divine life' is something that is often described as 'participatory metaphysics'.[157] A very popular narrative in recent scholarship is that Protestantism contributed to the abandonment of this metaphysical paradigm, which in the West is associated with the idea of the *analogia entis*.[158] After all, we cannot forget Barth's famous verdict that the *analogia entis* is the invention of the antichrist. I would like to argue that in order to really incorporate the doctrine of deification in our theological system we also need to espouse the metaphysical paradigm in the context of which it was developed and into which it makes sense.

The *analogia entis*, analogy of being, assumes that because of the relationship between God as creator and the world as His creation that creation provides us with a way of understanding God.

An alternative metaphysical paradigm which gives different meaning to the idea of 'union' with God has been proposed recently by several evangelical theologians. That puts forth the biblical concept of "covenant" as the controlling motif to describe the relationship between God and humanity.[159] According to Webster, 'a Reformed theology of participation' focuses on the economy of divine grace, which holds as its central principle that the 'history of God's dealings is 'covenantal' - an ordered moral history between personal agents (the uncreated God and his creatures) and not a process of diffusion of being'.[160] The subject of metaphysical presuppositions, as we have already stated, is very complex. Our intention has been merely to alert us to its significance and import in any discussion of deification.

The Role and the Nature of the 'Sacraments' of The Church

Another point that we need to take into account in our discussion is the role of the sacraments, namely what is referred to as 'sacramental realism'. For Orthodox theology, our participation in the life of God is attained chiefly through the sacraments, and in particular through baptism and the Eucharist. In his classic work, *The Mystical Theology of the Orthodox Church*, Lossky writes that, 'the sacramental unions which the Church offers us—even the eucharistic union, the most perfect of all— relate to our nature insofar as it is received into the person of Christ'.[161] Through our participation in the sacraments in the Church, 'our nature receives all the objective conditions of this union'.[162] Our spirit, namely the 'contemplative faculty by which man is able to seek God' in the Church and through the sacraments is 'united with baptismal grace, and through which grace enters into the heart, the centre of that human nature which is to be deified.'[163]

The Church then is, according to Gregory Palamas, the 'community of deification' (koinonia theoseos), since through its sacraments, it imparts the objective conditions for union with Christ.

As Evangelicals, we agree with the significance of the Holy Sacraments as means of grace, instituted by God for the purpose of our spiritual transformation. In his nine theses on deification, Evangelical scholar Robert Letham, begins by noting that 'the transformation that is part of union with Christ and called "theosis", comes to expression in, and is cultivated by, the Word and the Sacraments,'[164] explaining that the Eucharist is 'the point of union covenantally and personally between Christ and his people.'[165] At the same time, however, we observe that in the Orthodox approach the role of the Word of God and our faith are not given proper emphasis. The importance of faith is especially salient in the New Testament, as seen in the following representative texts. In Ephesians 3:17, Paul prays for Christ to dwell in the hearts of the recipients of his letter 'by faith'. In Galatians 3:1-2, he confronts the believers, saying, 'O foolish Galatians! Who has bewitched you? It was before your eyes that Jesus Christ was publicly portrayed as crucified. Let me ask you only this: Did you receive the Spirit by works of the law or by hearing with faith?' Finally, in Romans 10:9-11, we read, 'Because, if you confess with your mouth that Jesus is Lord and believe in your heart that God raised him from the dead, you will be saved. For with the heart one believes and is justified, and with the mouth one confesses and is saved. For the Scripture says, "Everyone who believes in him will not be put to shame".' Unfortunately the way in which many Orthodox theologians speak of participation in the Eucharist often comes across as something 'magical', almost akin to receiving a 'shot of divinity', as the well known Orthodox theologian, John Romanides, has famously bemoaned.

Synergistic Anthropology

Central to the Orthodox understanding of deification, as we have already said, is the distinction between image and likeness. Likeness concerns our calling, which was disrupted by the fall. The image of God, however, remains fully intact. While there may be other differences in content regarding the 'image', what all Orthodox theologians certainly agree on is that it entails the ideas of freedom and self-determination (*autexousion*). Man functions as an agent with free will, from which God must first receive consent, in order to act. This approach provokes many questions for the Evangelical. First of all, it seems to undermine the Scriptural witness concerning the sinful condition of fallen humanity, which is not described in a way that should lead us to such a positive and hopeful outlook. It also bypasses the significance of the divine initiative and the notion of grace as the unconditional offer that flows out of the lavishness of divine generosity.

Apart from matters of consent, the idea of synergy also pertains to the ascetic struggle that one must engage in, in order to reach deification. As Lossky writes, 'The whole human complex must become "spiritual" (πνευματικός), must acquire the "likeness".'[166] This, however, 'presupposes an unceasing vigilance of spirit and a constant effort of the will... when ardour slackens, resolution falters and grace remains inactive.'[167] That vigilance 'demands the full consciousness of the human person in all the degrees of its ascent toward perfect union.'[168]

The failure to distinguish between justification and sanctification leads to a synergistic understanding of salvation. As Letham astutely observes, this subject is 'the single most significant point of difference' between Eastern Orthodoxy and particularly the Reformed strand of Protestantism.[169]

ON THE OTHER HAND...

Despite these concerns and disagreements, there are nevertheless several helpful aspects of this doctrine, which we need to take into account. One such helpful aspect concerns the expanding of the horizon of the experience of salvation. What is the 'telos' unto which God justifies us in Christ by faith? Justification is the necessary condition for us to enter once again that which sin had prevented us from enjoying, namely our union with Christ and, through Him, our participation in the joy of the life of the Trinity. Although perhaps an oversimplification, we might say that while the Orthodox need to rediscover the 'beginning' of salvation, that is justification by faith, Evangelicals need to rediscover the 'end' (telos) of salvation, that is our union with Christ and our likeness with God, that is and in that sense our deification. In the last of his nine theses on deification, Letham notes the words of Calvin that, 'it is the intention of the gospel to make us sooner or later like God.'[170] An important point here is to see 'union' with God as eventually the overarching experience that covers the entirety of our salvation, from beginning to end. It is not simply an element in the '*ordo salutis*' but it is the experience that encompasses the totality of our redemption.[171]

Deification, moreover, does not only emphasise the 'telos' of our own personal salvation but the final purpose of all of existence and creation. It is worth taking seriously the criticism of Andrew Louth, when he writes that 'Western theologies tend to miss the trajectory from creation to deification, and thus tend to see the created order as little more than a background for the great drama of redemption, with the result that the Incarnation is seen simply as a means of redemption, the putting right of the Fall of Adam'.[172] Thus, the doctrine of deification causes us to see beyond our individual salvation and unto the plans of God for all of creation, to recapitulate all things in Christ.

AN EVANGELICAL REFORMULATION

In J. Todd Billings' work, *Calvin, Participation and the Gift*, we find the following paragraph from Calvin's commentary on John's gospel, explaining the verse 'that they all may be made one' from Jesus' high priestly prayer in John 17:21:

> To comprehend aright what it meant that Christ and the Father are one, take care not to deprive Christ of His person as Mediator. But consider Him rather as He is the Head of the Church, and join Him to His members. Thus the connection will best be preserved; that, if the unity of the Son with the Father is not to be fruitless and useless, its power must be diffused through the whole body of believers. From this, too, we infer that we are one with Christ; not because He transfuses His substance into us, but because by the power of His Spirit He communicates to us His life and all the blessings He has received from the Father.[173]

In the above quote, we encounter the building blocks, with which to shape an Evangelical reformulation of the doctrine of deification. First we see that our union with Christ is emphasised, though not in the sense of a 'transfusion of His substance', but 'by the power of His Spirit'. The term 'substance' as Calvin explains, refers to the 'life and all the blessings that Christ has received from the Father'. This power (*energeia*)[174] of Christ is not given to the few but to all believers through the Holy Spirit. This experience is not therefore the endpoint of a process, which only a few are able to complete, but 'the way in which believers are deified in redemption'. Billings, summarising Calvin's theology on the concept of the 'participation' of the believer in Christ, states that, 'Calvin offers his own appropriation of the biblical and patristic theme of participation, strongly emphasizing a Johannine theology of "indwelling" along with a Pauline soteriology of sin and forgiveness'.[175] He concludes, saying, 'For Calvin, the path toward participation in God necessarily involves the reception of the Father's free pardon as believers are united to Christ through faith, by the Spirit'.[176] The first blessing of our union with Christ is our justification, an idea that does not carry only a forensic sense but a deeply participatory-experiential one also. Calvin finds an analogue of this experience of justification 'in Christ' before God in the story of Jacob, when he is 'clothed' with the garments and the characteristic aroma of Esau, and thus receives the blessing of the Father. He writes, 'And this is indeed the truth, for in order that we may appear before God's face unto salvation we must smell sweetly with his odour, and our vices must be covered and buried by his perfection'.[177]

6

HOW ARE WE SAVED?

Kallistos Ware, Metropolitan of Diokleia, relates
something that happened to him in the USA. As he was
travelling one day by train, someone approached him
and asked him, 'Are you saved?' Most Evangelicals feel
quite comfortable with this question. Ware, however, was
taken aback. How should he respond? In his book, *How
are we saved?*[178] he attempts to present the Orthodox
answer to this pertinent question. We have chosen to
close this short overview of Orthodox theology with an
examination of this small book because it is here that we
come to the 'so what' of our study. Is there actually a real
difference between the Orthodox and the Evangelical
answer to this question, or 'do all roads lead to Rome'?

THE ORTHODOX WAY

In short, Ware's answer to the question, 'are you saved?' is, 'I trust by God's mercy and grace I am being saved' (p. 4). He prefers the use of the continuous present here in order to show that the experience of salvation is not definitive and final but open-ended and progressive. He believes this for two reasons. The first is that, while the victory of Christ over sin and death is indeed complete and definitive, my 'subjective, personal participation' in Christ's victory or else, my 'personal incorporation in Christ' is 'incomplete' (p. 4). There is, also, another reason for the use of continuous present and that is, as Ware insists, that 'for my part I retain continuing freedom of choice, the ability to refuse as well as to obey' (p. 4).

In Orthodox theology, therefore, the salvation is 'not a single event in that person's past but an ongoing process' (p. 6) It is a journey that has not yet reached its destination. On this journey, Jesus is our 'inseparable companion' (p. 6). Since it is ongoing, however, 'I cannot speak as if its successful termination were already certain and secure' (p. 6).

As we have already seen in this discussion, the idea of freedom of will of humanity plays a very significant role. Ware writes that the Orthodox Church believes 'that even in their sinful and fallen state human beings still possess the power of free choice', the Orthodox Church sees salvation in terms of *synergeia* or 'cooperation' between divine grace and human freedom. In St. Paul's words, 'We are fellow-workers (*synergoi*) with God'

(1 Cor. 3:9) (p. 34). What man freely contributes, he explains, is 'our voluntary participation' (p. 34) in God's saving action.

AN EVANGELICAL RESPONSE

THE ORTHODOX ARE NOT ROMAN CATHOLIC

The most important thing that Evangelicals must understand is that Orthodox are not Roman Catholics! We must bear in mind that the idea of meritorious good works is foreign to their theology. Ware, quoting Lossky, writes that, 'The notion of merit is foreign to the Eastern tradition... Even though we affirm that human free will is an essential condition in no way does this signify that salvation can be earned or deserved' (p. 38). We must also note that in Orthodox theology, the soteriological question is not formulated around the concepts of faith and works, but of divine grace and human freedom. Salvation is the fruit of synergy between divine grace and human freedom.

In this sense, according to Ware, it is not possible to conceive of synergy as a matter of quantity, in the sense that God contributes a certain percentage and humans the rest. Indeed, Ware insists, and we must listen carefully to him, that, 'it is totally and entirely an act of divine grace and in it we remain totally and entirely free. It remains always the free gift of God' (p. 38).

He further explains that 'our free will presupposes from the start the presence of divine grace and without this "prevenient" grace we could not begin to exercise our will aright' (p. 42). The term, 'prevenient grace' may surprise us but it needs to be especially appreciated by the Evangelicals.

SALVATION AS PROCESS

One of the most important features in Ware's presentation is his conception of salvation as a 'journey'. We encounter the same idea of an ongoing process in Russell's definition of deification.

> Theosis is our restoration as persons to integrity and wholeness by participation in Christ through the Holy Spirit, in a process which is initiated in this world through our life of ecclesial communion and moral striving and finds ultimate fulfilment in our union with the Father — all within the broad context of the divine economy.[179]

The understanding of salvation exclusively as a process derives from various presuppositions, which we believe to be problematic and will examine below.

The Nature of Salvation

If the nature of salvation is 'deification', then the question 'are you saved?' is akin to asking someone if they have been 'deified'. Who could dare answer this question in the affirmative? Salvation has to be a continual ascent towards God with the ultimate goal of union with Him. Fairbairn's observation on the two models of salvation is instructive here.[180] He notes that there are two competing views of sin and salvation both found in the patristic tradition. He describes the one as a three-act scheme and the other a two-act scheme of salvation. The first views salvation involving three key acts or movements: creation, fall and restoration. The other sees two, creation and elevation. In the two-act scheme, God creates people with potential, not perfection, and gives them a calling to ascend and be united with Him. The whole notion of salvation in this second scheme has at its centre, by its very nature, the idea of process and movement towards a goal. Although both models can be found in texts of early Christianity, it is the second which appears to have defined Orthodox theology and soteriology. Evangelical theology, on the other hand, believes that the three-act scheme is consistent with the biblical narrative. The important thing in this approach is that as the fall is an event which creates a new reality, so salvation is also a similar event which brings forth a new situation. Metaphors such as 'adoption' or 'reconciliation', and of course 'justification' convey a clear sense of finality and completeness.

A Failure to Distinguish
Between Justification and Sanctification

The most fundamental difference between Evangelicals of all persuasion, and the approach of the Orthodox Church, is that the Orthodox, according to Ware, 'do not have in view any sharp differentiation between justification and sanctification' (p. 66). Ware maintains that 'salvation… is not a single event in our past life but an ongoing process of growth in Christ' (p. 66).

As Evangelicals, of course, we accept that our growth in Christ is an ongoing process. However, we call this process 'sanctification' and we distinguish it from the experience of 'justification'. All Evangelicals accept the present continuous, namely that 'we are being saved'; we are being saved from the power and corruption of sin. At the same time, however, we also emphasise the present perfect, namely that 'we have been saved' from our guilt and the penalty of sin, referring to an experience that took place in the past, with lasting effect into the present.

Calvin writes in his *Institutes*, 'By partaking of Him, we…receive a double grace: namely, that being reconciled to God through Christ's blamelessness, we may have in heaven instead of a judge a gracious Father; and secondly, that sanctified by Christ's Spirit we may cultivate blamelessness and purity of life'.[181] Calvin's language is worth taking note of here, as he explicitly uses the language of participation in Christ, rather than the language of a forensic settlement, as many Orthodox, including Ware, falsely accuse Evangelicals of employing exclusively to define salvation. We see here Calvin emphasising that our participation in Christ has a twofold benefit. The first is our reconciliation with God—and here we might also include other New Testament ideas such as regeneration, adoption, translation from the kingdom of darkness to the kingdom of light, et al. These all describe a complete and final experience. The second benefit concerns our sanctification. The two are not separate, but rather distinct. Thus, I may say that I am being saved (from the power and the consequences of sin) but also that I have been saved (from the burden, the curse and the guilt of sin).[182]

The Nature of the Work of Christ on the Cross

As we have already seen, for most Orthodox theologians, the central meaning of Christ's work on the cross is His victory over death and sin. The concepts of atonement, substitution, and forgiveness are either secondary or completely absent, something Ware concedes when he says that, 'the Orthodox Church has never formally endorsed any particular theory of atonement' (p. 49). This has repercussions for the way we understand salvation. If the only thing that the cross of Christ offers me victory over is sin, then of course it is impossible for me, during the course of my earthly life, to say that I am saved. Who could ever claim to have completely defeated sin and death in his or her own life? If, however, we approach the work of Christ, espousing the aspect of forgiveness and atonement, then salvation can indeed be viewed and grasped as something certain, final and completed.

WHY THE DOCTRINE OF JUSTIFICATION MATTERS

Ware admits something that is very revealing. Discussing the topic of justification, he does not differentiate it from sanctification. He, moreover, notes that in his popular work *The Orthodox Church* the word 'justification' does not appear even once, though 'this was not a deliberate omission' (p. 66). It is obvious that, for Ware and many other Orthodox theologians, the idea of justification is peripheral, even unnecessary in order to understand God's salvific economy. Why then, do we Evangelicals insist on it? Are we fixating on a legal fiction invented by a guilt-ridden Luther? In closing, I would like to note why I believe that the absence of this doctrine constitutes a significant oversight in Orthodox theology.

'Good works' through the back door

The first reason we emphasise justification is because its absence unavoidably introduces 'good works' as an important component in the process of salvation. In his book, Ware is very careful when speaking of synergy to constrain it to the idea of human consent. This idea of consent is understood primarily as participation in the sacramental life of the Church. However, if there is no distinction between a final and objective experience (justification) from an ongoing and subjective process (sanctification), at the end our effort and good works contribute to our salvation. Lossky explains that the way to union with God 'presupposes an unceasing vigilance of spirit and a constant effort of the will'.[183] Though, as we already saw, Lossky rejects any notion of merit nevertheless he insists that 'fasts, vigils, prayers, alms, and other good works done in the name of Christ... are the means whereby we acquire the Holy Spirit'.[184] He further explains it is only good works done in the name of Christ that 'win us the grace of God in this present life'.[185] It seems to me, that from the moment one does not distinguish between justification and sanctification, it is inevitable for works, as part of the pursuit of salvation, to enter by the back door.

That confusion explains, I believe, no matter what theologians say, the idea that our good works contribute to our salvation, which is so widespread among the lay orthodox believers. As an example of this, one may think about the teachings on 'aerial toll houses'. The basic idea is that on the third day after death, the soul goes before twenty demonic spirits, who accuse it regarding various sins into which they have attempted to lead it. These are the twenty tolls through which the believer passes, debunking the accusations by countering them with corresponding good works that he or she has done. The reason why the extremely popular memorial prayer for the dead takes place on the third day is so that the prayers of the faithful might help the soul of the departed during this frightful process. Although this teaching and still ongoing popular practice has been harshly criticised by various Orthodox theologians,[186] it has been supported by others, most notably by Seraphim Rose[187] and Metropolitan Hierotheos Vlachos.[188]

The Psychology of Christian Experience

At one point in his analysis, Ware explains that while we have confidence in the work of Christ, we don't have the same confidence in our own faithfulness. Thus, he explains, 'Conscious as I am of my human frailty, I remain between hope and fear right up to the very gates of death' (p. 5). Protestants affirm both of these truths, but with a very different outworking: although I do not have confidence in my own faithfulness, nevertheless, or perhaps precisely for this reason, I have confidence in the work of Christ. If we reverse the order, then naturally we must always live in a state of 'limbo', trying to balance hope and fear. In other words, one never knows and one can never be sure. Reformed insistence upon the forensic, *extra nos* basis of justification provides the sinner with a sense of assurance of her acceptance before God, and offers her consolation in the midst of her ongoing struggle with sin.[189] This assurance is expressed best through the opening question and answer of the *Heidelberg Catechism*:

Q: What is your only comfort in life and death?

A: That I am not my own, but belong with body and soul, both in life and in death, to my faithful Saviour Jesus Christ. He has fully paid for all my sins with His precious blood, and has set me free from all the power of the devil. He also preserves me in such a way that without the will of my heavenly Father not a hair can fall from my head; indeed, all things must work together for my salvation. Therefore, by His Holy Spirit He also assures me of eternal life and makes me heartily willing and ready from now on to live for Him.

We have already referred to the Jesus Prayer. It is worth looking at its content, 'O Jesus Christ, Son of God, have mercy on me, a sinner'. This prayer reflects a true facet of the Christian experience concerning the daily, unceasing struggle against sin. However, the plea to have mercy must be informed and complemented by the corresponding truth that I received mercy. Only then shall we pray like the apostle Paul (1 Tim. 1:12-16):

> I thank him who has given me strength, Christ Jesus our Lord, because he judged me faithful, appointing me to his service, though formerly I was a blasphemer, persecutor, and insolent opponent. *But I received mercy* because I had acted ignorantly in unbelief, and the grace of our Lord overflowed for me with the faith and love that are in Christ Jesus. The saying is trustworthy and deserving of full acceptance, that Christ Jesus came into the world to save sinners, of whom I am the foremost. *But I received mercy* for this reason, that in me, as the foremost, Jesus Christ might display his perfect patience as an example to those who were to believe in him for eternal life.

FURTHER READING

Evangelical Resources

Donald Fairbairn, *Eastern Orthodoxy Through Western Eyes* (Louisville: Westminster John Knox, 2002).

Robert Letham, *Through Western Eyes: Eastern Orthodoxy: A Reformed Perspective* (Fearn: Christian Focus, 2010).

James J. Stamoolis, ed. *Three Views on Eastern Orthodoxy and Evangelicalism* (Counterpoints Series) (Grand Rapids: Zondervan, 2004).

Eastern Orthodox Sources

Andrew Louth, *Introducing Eastern Orthodox Theology* (Downers Grove: InterVarsity, 2013).

Vladimir Lossky, *The Mystical Theology of the Eastern Church* (Crestwood: St Vladimir's Seminary, 1976).

Kallistos Ware, *The Orthodox Church* (London: Penguin, 1997).

John Anthony McGuckin, *The Orthodox Church: An Introduction to its History, Doctrine and Spiritual Culture* (Oxford: Blackwell, 2008).

Norman Russell, *Fellow Workers with God: Orthodox Thinking on Theosis* (Yonkers: Saint Vladimir's, 2009).

ENDNOTES

1   Donald Fairbairn, *Eastern Orthodoxy Through Western Eyes* (Louisville: Westminster John Knox, 2002).

2   Robert Letham, *Through Western Eyes: Eastern Orthodoxy: A Reformed Perspective* (Fearn: Christian Focus, 2010).

3   For helpful document providing a basic definition of the name 'Evangelical' see https://www.lausanne.org/content/covenant/lausanne-covenant

4   In this regard, it is interesting to note the following comment by David Bentley Hart, that 'between Eastern Orthodox and Reformed theology there are some differences so vast that no reconciliation is possible'. In David Bentley Hart, *The Doors of the Sea* (Grand Rapids; Cambridge: Eerdmans, 2005), 94.

5   Pseudo-Dionysius Areopagite, *The Divine Names and Mystical Theology*, Translated by John D. Jones, (Milwaukee: Marquette University, 1980), 211.

6   Andrew Louth, *Introducing Eastern Orthodox Theology* (Downers Grove: InterVarsity, 2013), 123.

7   Andrew Louth, 'Tradition and the Tacit' in *Discerning the Mystery: An Essay on the Nature of Theology* (Oxford: Clarendon, 1983), 89.

8   Ibid., 86.

9   Louth, *Introducing Eastern Orthodox Theology*, 123.

10   Lossky more than any other modern theologian is connected with what Sarah Coakley called the 'recent upsurge of interest in the mysterious early sixth-century author, "Dionysius the Areopagite"'. More on that and the post-modern 'apophatic rage' in Sarah Coakley's article 'Re-thinking Dionysius the Areopagite', *Modern Theology*, 24:4, October 2008, 531-540.

11   Vladimir Lossky, *The Mystical Theology of the Eastern Church* (Crestwood: St Vladimir's Seminary, 1976), 25.

12   In the same icon we notice the disciples depicted in the night, ascending toward the revelation of the light.

13   Lossky, *Mystical Theology*, 43.

14   A. N. Williams, 'The Transcendence of Apophaticism' in *Theological Theology: Essays in Honour of John Webster*, ed. R. David Nelson, Darren Sarisky and Justin Stratis (London: Bloomsbury T&T Clark, 2015), 319.

15   Vladimir Lossky, 'Tradition and Traditions' in *In The Image and Likeness of God*, ed. John H. Erickson and Thomas E. Bird (Crestwood: St. Vladimir's, 1974), 161-2.

16   See also among others, Timothy Ward, *Words of Life: Scripture as the Living and Active Word of God* (Downers Grove: IVP Academic, 2009).

17   Olivier Boulnois, 'Les Noms Divins, Négation ou Transcendance?', *Revue De Théologie et de Philosophie*, 150 (2019): 315-333.

18   In the prayer we quoted at the beginning of our chapter we have the prefix hyper in ten words.

19   *On the Divine Names* I, 1.

20   'Perverso rationis amore' in Augustine, *De Trinitate* 1.1.1.

21   Aquinas, *Summa Theologica* I, Q 1., translated by the Fathers of the English Dominican Province (New York: Benzinger, 1947).

22   A.N. Williams, 'The Transcendence of Apophaticism', 334.

23   As quoted in Carl R. Trueman, *Luther on the Christian Life* (Wheaton: Crossway, 2015), 45-46.

24   Georges Florovsky, Bible, Church, Tradition: An Eastern Orthodox View, vol. 1 in the *Collected Works of Georges Florovsky* (Belmont: Nordland, 1972).

25   George Florovsky, 'The Catholicity of the Church', in Bible, Church, Tradition, pp. 46–7.

26   Vladimir Lossky, 'Tradition and Traditions', 132.

27   Andrew Louth, 'Tradition and the Tacit' in *Discerning the Mystery: An Essay on the Nature of Theology* (Wichita: Eighth Day, 2007), 86.

28   Ibid., 88.

29   Ibid., 95.

30   Kallistos Ware, *The Orthodox Church* (London: Penguin, 1997), 196.

31   For an effort to correct this distortion see Michael Allen and Scott R. Swain, *Reformed Catholicity: The Promise of Retrieval for Theology and Biblical Interpretation* (Grand Rapids: Baker Academic, 2015), especially their discussion on an ecclesial understanding of sola Scriptura in pp. 49 - 70.

32   Aristotle Papanikolaou, 'Tradition as Reason and Practice: Amplifying Contemporary Orthodox Theology in Conversation with Alisdair MacIntyre' *SVTQ* 59:1 (2015), 93.

33   Elizabeth Behr-Sigel also raises the same question: 'How can we distinguish the authentic, living Tradition of the Church from the traditions, in the plural, that are not bad in themselves but are relative to their historical situation?' In Michael Plekon and Sarah E. Hinlicky eds., *Discerning the Times: The Vision of Elisabeth Behr-Sigel* (Crestwood: St Vladimir's Seminary, 2001), 90.

34   The title of the paper was 'The Fathers and the Concept of Tradition' and it was delivered in Athens on May 16th, 2013.

35   Paul L. Gavrilyuk, 'The Orthodox Renaissance,' *First Things* (December 2012), 34.

36   For a detailed discussion of all these complex issues in Orthodox Ecclesiology see Cyril Hovorun, *Scaffolds of the Church, Towards Poststructural Ecclesiology* (Eugene: Cascade, 2017), 48.

37   Paul L. Gavrilyuk, 'The Epistemological Contours of Florovsky's Neopatristic Theology,' *Journal of Eastern Christian Studies* 69 (1-4), 13.

38   Emphasis mine. Gallaher, suggests that Florovsky, ironically, that is despite his critical attitude towards the West, has here been influenced by such authors as Möhler and Schelling. In Brandon Gallaher, 'Waiting for the Barbarians,' *Modern Theology* 27:4 (October 2011), 670.

39   Phrase used by Fr. Florensky and quoted by Louth, 'The Fathers and The Concept of Tradition', p.11.

40   John Anthony McGuckin, *The Orthodox Church: An Introduction to its History, Doctrine and Spiritual Culture* (Oxford: Blackwell, 2008).

41   William R. Schoedel, *A Commentary of the Letters of Ignatius of Antioch*, Hermeneia (Philadelphia: Fortress Press 1985), 197.

42   Ibid., 238.

43   The same is true also for Arius and his argumentation. The basic ground of contention between Arius and Athanasius is '"the sense of Scripture" viewed as a whole', see Rowan Williams, *Arius: Heresy and Tradition*, rev. ed. (Grand Rapids: Eerdmans, 2001), 249.

44   William R. Schoedel, *A Commentary of the Letters of Ignatius of Antioch*, 238.

45   Michael J. Kruger, *Canon Revisited: Establishing the Origins and Authority of the New Testament Books* (Wheaton: Crossway, 2012), 45.

46   John Webster, 'The Dogmatic Location of the Canon' in *Word and Church, Essays in Christian Dogmatics* (Edinburgh: T.&T. Clark, 2001), 40.

47   Ibid.

48   Karl Barth, *Church Dogmatics*, vol. I, part. 1 (Edinburgh: T.&T. Clark, 1975, 2nd ed.), 104.

49   Ibid., 101.

50   John Webster, 'Scripture, Church and Canon' in *Holy Scripture: A Dogmatic Sketch* (Cambridge: Cambridge University, 2003).

51   Karl Barth, *Church Dogmatics*, vol. I, part 2 (Edinburgh: T.&T. Clark, 1956), 581.

52   Ibid.

53   Ibid., 582.

54   John Webster, 'The Dogmatic Location of the Canon' in *Word and Church, Essays in Christian Dogmatics* (Edinburgh: T.&T. Clark, 2001), 9.

55   Ibid.

56   *Luther Works*, 33, ed. Philip S. Watson, general editor Helmut T. Lehmann (Philadelphia: Fortress, 1972), 294.

57   David Bentley Hart, *The Hidden and the Manifest* (Grand Rapids: Eerdmans, 2017), 325. He means 'Eastern Orthodox Christians'.

58   Ibid., 139.

59   Gerald Bray, 'Original Sin in Patristic Thought', *Churchman* 108.1 (1994), 47.

60   Stavros Yagazoglou, 'Sin, Freedom and Self-Determination', *Synaxis* vol. 144 (2017), 41 - 54 (in Greek, translation mine).

61   On this point Yagazoglou differs from many Orthodox theologians who argue that mortality is a consequence of the fall. See previous chapter.

62   This is a phrase used extensively in various patristic writings. For a recent appropriation see among others, Panayiotis Nellas, *Deification in Christ: Orthodox Perspectives on the Nature of the Human Person*, trans. Norman Russell (Crestwood: St Vladimir's Seminary Press, 1987), 178-88.

63   John Zizioulas, 'Man the Priest of Creation', A. Walker and C. Carras (eds.) *Living Orthodoxy in the Modern World* (London: SPCK, 1996).

64   Stavros Yagazoglou, 'Human Self-determination and Freedom. Theological Anthropology in the Orthodox Tradition and the teaching of Martin Luther', *Theologia*, vol. 1 (2019), 133 (in Greek).

65   John Zizioulas, 'Preserving God's Creation: Lecture Three', *King's Theological Review* vol. 13 (1990), 2.

66   Ware, *The Orthodox Church*, 219.

67   This term is being used by Florovsky who describes original sin as 'not merely a choice of the wrong direction but rather a refusal that man ascend to God, a desertion from God's service', George Florovsky, *Creation and Redemption* (Belmont: Nordland, 1972), 95.

68   Ware, *The Orthodox Church*, 220.

69   Ibid., 223.

70   Ibid.

71   Ibid.

72   According to Engel, 'Calvin explicitly says that sin destroys, extinguishes, erases, rubs out, and effaces the image in humankind'. Mary Potter Engel, *John Calvin's Perspectival Anthropology* (Eugene, OR: Wipe and Stock Publishers, 1988), 56.

73   As Luther does, see David Cairns, *The Image of God in Man* (New York: Philosophical Library, 1953), 124.

74   Michael Horton, *The Christian Faith, A Systematic Theology for Pilgrims on the Way* (Grand Rapids, Michigan: Zondervan, 2011), 437. That follows the basic idea the whereas we affirm that 'the whole spectrum of created reality is good, so Reformed theologians have affirmed that every nook and cranny of creation has been distorted by sin' in R. Michael Allen, *Reformed Theology* (New York: T&T Clark, 2010), 160.

75   Mentioned in Ian A. McFarland, *In Adam's Fall, A Meditation on the Christian Doctrine of Original Sin* (Malden, MA:Wiley-Blackwell, 2010), 4.

76   Ibid., 33.

77   Ware, *The Orthodox Church*, 224.

78   A characteristic, though extreme example of that is the book of the well known Greek theologian - philosopher Christos Yannaras *Fall - Judgement - Hell or the Forensic Undermining of Ontology* (Athens: Ikaros, 2017).

79   Michael F. Bird, *Evangelical Theology* (Grand Rapids, Michigan: Zondervan, 2013), 672-4.

80   Gerald Bray, 'Sin in Historical Theology', *Fallen: A Theology of Sin,* Christopher W. Morgan and Robert A. Peterson eds. (Wheaton, Illinois: Crossway, 2013), 168.

81   Ware, *The Orthodox Church*, 223.

82   Of course this is borne out not only in our experience, but also in the Word of God.

83   Cf. John Behr, *The Mystery of Christ: Life in Death* (New York: St Vladimir's, 2006), 112.

84   Michael Horton, *The Christian Faith: A Systematic Theology*, 426.

85   Robert Jenson as quoted in Horton, Ibid., 426.

86   Douglas Moo, 'Sin in Paul' in *Fallen: A Theology of Sin*, ed. Christopher W. Morgan and Robert A. Peterson (Crossway), 125.

87   John Behr, *Irenaeus of Lyons: Identifying Christianity* (Oxford: Oxford University, 2013), 145.

88   McFarland, *In Adam's Fall*, 63.

89   Ibid., 48.

90   The quotations that follow are from St. Athanasius, *On the Incarnation*, Popular Patristics Series no.3 (Crestwood, New York: St. Vladimir's Seminary Press, 1996).

91   Keith Getty, 'In Christ Alone'.

92   Isaac Watts, 'Jesus My Great Priest'.

93   Yagazoglou, 'Sin, Freedom and Self-Determination'.

94   Ware, *The Orthodox Church*, 225.

95   Vladimir Lossky, *In the Image and Likeness of God*, John H. Erickson and Thomas E. Bird eds. (Crestwood: St Vladimir's Seminary, 1974), 97.

96   Ibid., 98.

97   George Florovsky, *Creation and Redemption*, vol. 3 (Belmont: Nordland, 1976), 96.

98   Gustav Aulén, *Christus Victor: A Historical Study of the Three Main Types of the Idea of the Atonement*, trans. A. G. Herbert (New York: Macmillan, 1931).

99   As the above mentioned famous Byzantine Easter song concludes.

100   Lossky, *In the Image and Likeness of God*, 98.

101   Ibid., 104.

102   Ware, *The Orthodox Church*, 228.

103   For more see, 'The Place of the Cross among the Inseparable Operations of the Trinity' by Adonis Vidu in *Locating Atonement: Explorations in Constructive Dogmatics*, Oliver D. Crisp and Fred Sanders, Eds. (Grand Rapids: Zondervan, 2015).

104   Jeremy R. Treat, *The Crucified King: Atonement and Kingdom in Biblical and Systematic Theology* (Grand Rapids: Zondervan, 2014). Also, Michael Horton, *Lord and Servant* (Lousville: Westminster John Knox,

2005) and more specifically the chapter 'Suffering Servant: Challenges to Sacrificial Atonement', 178-208. On the other hand, James R. Payton's recent book *The Victory of the Cross: Salvation in Eastern Orthodoxy* (Downers Grove: IVP Academics, 2019) is very disappointing. His work is marked by a complete absence of any kind of creative reconstruction of an atonement theology that reconstitutes these various aspects of the cross into an enriched and fuller formulation.

105 See also Romans 5 and 6, 8:1-12, 1 Corinthians 15:55-57, Galatians 1:4.

106 Fleming Rutledge, *The Crucifixion: Understanding the Death of Jesus Christ* (Grand Rapids: Eerdmans, 2015), 209.

107 Quoted in Lossky, *In the Image*, 29.

108 David Bentley Hart, 'A Gift Exceeding Every Debt: An Eastern Orthodox Appreciation of Anselm's Cur Deus Homo', *Pro Ecclesia* Vol. VII, No.3, 339.

109 Robert Letham, *The Work of Christ* (Leicester: Inter-Varsity, 1993), 133.

110 Simon Gathercole, *Defending Substitution: An Essay on Atonement in Paul* (Acadia Studies in Bible and Theology, Grand Rapids: Baker Academic, 2015), 15.

111 To those we may add 2 Corinthians 5:21, Romans 8:1-3, Galatians 3:13, Hebrews 9:12, 16, 1 John 2:2, 4:10, 1 Peter 2:24, 3:18.

112 Rutledge, Ibid., 75.

113 Calvin, *Institutes* 2.16.6.

114 Giorgio Agamben, *Pilate and Jesus*, Adam Kotsko translator (Stanford, California: Stanford University, 2015), 39.

115 Rutledge, 148.

116 David Bentley Hart, 'A Gift Exceeding Every Debt', 346.

117 Miroslav Volf, *Free of Charge: Giving and Forgiving in a Culture Stripped of Grace* (Grand Rapids: Zondervan, 2005), 143.

118 Rutledge, 130.

119 Miroslav Volf, *Exclusion and Embrace* (Nashville: Abingdon, 1996), 297.

120 Rutledge, 131.

121 Ibid.

122   Garry Williams calls this example 'a travesty of penal substitution' (in 'Penal Substitution — A Response to Recent Criticisms' *The Atonement Debate*, ed. Derek Tidball, David Hilborn and Justin Thacker (Grand Rapids: Zondervan, 2008), 179.

123   Adonis Vidu, 'The Place of the Cross among the Inseparable Operations of the Trinity' *Locating Atonement: Explorations in Constructive Dogmatics*, Oliver D. Crisp and Fred Sanders, Eds. (Grand Rapids: Zondervan, 2015).

124   John Stott, *The Cross of Christ*, 2nd edition (Leicester: IVP, 1989), 151.

125   Volf, *Free of Charge*, 145.

126   Stanley E. Porter, Καταλλάσσω in *Ancient Greek Literature, with Reference to the Pauline Writings* (Cordova: Ediciones El Almendro, 1994).

127   David Bentley Hart, *The Doors of the Sea* (Grand Rapids/Cambridge: Eerdmans, 2005).

128   'Nur der leidende Gott kann helfen' (Only the suffering God can help), Dietrich Bonhoeffer, *Letters and Papers from Prison* (London: SCM, 1967), 3rd. ed., 361.

129   Ware, *The Orthodox Church*, 236.

130   Ibid., 231.

131   Norman Russell, *The Doctrine of Deification in the Greek Patristic Tradition* (Oxford: Oxford University, 2004) and also his more accessible book *Fellow Workers with God: Orthodox Thinking on Theosis* (Yonkers: Saint Vladimir's, 2009).

132   This is a phrase coined and popularized by the well-known Greek Orthodox theologian Nikos Matsoukas.

133   Georgios Mantzaridis, *The Deification of Man: St. Gregory Palamas and the Orthodox Tradition* (Contemporary Greek Theologians Series , No 2), (Crestwood: SVS, 1984), 96.

134   Robert Letham, *Union with Christ: In Scripture, History and Theology* (Phillipsburg: P&R, 2011).

135   For the view that wants Luther to have a developed theology of deification cf. Carl E. Braaten and Robert W. Jenson, *Union with Christ: the New Finnish Interpretation of Luther* (Grand Rapids:

Eerdmans, 1998). For a different view cf. Carl R. Trueman, *The Wages of Spin* (Fearn: Christian Focus, 2004), 129-148.

136   Panayiotis Nellas, *Deification in Christ: Orthodox Perspectives on the Nature of the Human Person*, transl. Norman Russell (Crestwood: St Vladimir's Seminary, 1987), 115.

137   More on that in Letham, *Union with Christ*, 85-128.

138   We use this term following Russell though it may be misleading. Ware explains that 'the mystical union between God and humans is a true union, yet in this union Creator and creature do not become fused into a single being' (*Orthodox Church*, 232). At the same time, though, things can be a bit confusing as for example with the classic definition of deification found in Dionysius' Ecclesiastical Hierarchy (3.13) as being 'united to His most Divine Life by our assimilation to it, as far as possible'. The word 'assimilation' (ἀφομοίωσις) demands expounding!

139   Michael Horton, *The Christian Faith: A Systematic Theology for Pilgrims on the Way*, 692. In the same line is also N. Russell's definition, 'Theosis is our restoration as persons to integrity and wholeness by participation in Christ through the Holy Spirit, in a process which is initiated in this world through our life of ecclesial communion and moral striving and finds ultimate fulfilment in our union with the Father — all within the broad context of the divine economy' (Russell, *Fellow Workers with God*, 21).

140   Dietrich Bonhoeffer, *Ethics* (New York: Simon & Schuster), 73.

141   Andrew Louth, 'The Place of Theosis in Orthodox Theology' in Michael J. Christensen and Jeffrey A. Wittung eds., *Partakers of the Divine Nature* (Grand Rapids: Baker Academic, 2008), 39.

142   Jordan Cooper describes this approach 'neoplatonic' and distinguishes it from the version that one encounters in Irenaeus and Athanasius. In Jordan Cooper, *Christification: A Lutheran Approach to Theosis* (Eugene: Wipf and Stock, 2014), 11.

143   Pseudo-Dionysius Areopagite, *The Divine Names and Mystical Theology*, Translated by John D. Jones, (Milwaukee: Marquette University, 1980), 211.

144   See also in Palamas, '…Those who seek to attain it, they must gain the mastery over every sensual pleasure, completely rejecting the passions…' Palamas, *The Triads*, C 6, 49.

145   Palamas, Homily 2, PG 151, 20C, in Mantzaridis, *Deification of Man*, 89.

146   For more on the techniques of this prayer see Kallistos Ware, *The Jesus Prayer* (New ed., London: Catholic Truth Society, 2017).

147   Vladimir Lossky, *The Mystical Theology of the Eastern Church* (Crestwood: St Vladimir's Seminary, 1957), 209.

148   See for example Ioannis Romanides, *Patristic Theology*, ed. Monk Damascenos (Thessalonika: Parakatathiki, 2004), 49 (in Greek).

149   The lecture can be found in http://old.imd.gr/articles/left/video/504. For an English translation cf. *Sobornost* 34:1, 2012, 5-15.

150   Ware, *The Orthodox Church*, 236.

151   For a characteristic example see Veli-Matti Kärkkäinen, *One With God: Salvation as Deification and Justification* (Collegeville: Liturgical, 2004), also his article 'The Doctrine of Theosis and its Ecumenical Potential,' *Sobornost* 23, no 2 (2001): 45-77.

152   Andrew Louth, 'The Place of Theosis in Orthodox Theology', 32-44.

153   Paul L. Gavrilyuk, 'The Retrieval of Deification: How a Once-Despised Archaism Became an Ecumenical Desideratum', *Modern Theology* 25:4 (2009), 647-659.

154   Gösta Hallonsten, 'Theosis in Recent Research: A Renewal of Interest and a Need for Clarity', in Michael J. Christensen and Jeffrey A. Wittung, eds., *Partakers of the Divine Nature: The History and Development of Deification in the Christian Traditions* (Madison and Teaneck: Fairleigh Dickenson University, 2007).

155   Dumitru Staniloae, *Theology and the Church*, trans. Robert Barringer (Crestwood: St. Vladimir's Seminary, 1980), 116.

156   A. N. Williams, *The Ground of Union: Deification in Aquinas and Palamas* (Oxford: Oxford University, 1999), 32.

157   Gavrilyuk, *The Retrieval of Deification*, 650.

158   See for example, Brad S. Gregory, *The Unintended Reformation: How a Religious Revolution Secularized Society* (Boston: Harvard University, 2012).

159   Michael Horton, 'Participation, Analogy, and Covenant', in *Radical Orthodoxy and the Reformed Tradition*, pp. 108–9. Here one may also note the work of N. T. Wright ('Jesus and the Identity of

God', *Ex Auditu* 14, 1998, and also his *History and Eschatology: Jesus and the Promise of Natural Theology*, London: SPCK, 2019) and Richard Bauckham (*God Crucified: Monotheism and Christology in the New Testament*, Grand Rapids: Eerdmans, 1999) which puts forth a criticism to the adoption of a Platonic metaphysical paradigm and the abandonment of the context and worldview of biblical narrative or, in other words, for the 'conceptual shift from Jewish to Greek categories' (*God Crucified*, 78).

160   John Webster, 'Perfection and Participation', in Thomas Josephe White, ed., *The Analogy of Being: Invention of the Antichrist or the Wisdom of God?* (Grand Rapids: Eerdmans, 2011), 386.

161   Lossky, *Mystical Theology*, 138.

162   Ibid.

163   Ibid., 201.

164   Robert Letham, *Systematic Theology* (Wheaton: Crossway, 2019), 707.

165   Ibid.

166   Lossky, *Mystical Theology*, 201.

167   Ibid, 202.

168   Ibid.

169   Robert Letham, *Through Western Eyes: Eastern Orthodoxy: A Reformed Perspective* (Fearn: Christian Focus, 2010), 78.

170   Letham, *Systematic Theology*, 707. He further explains that 'Calvin goes on to say that "nature" here means not essence but kind; we participate not in the being of God but in his attributes, his qualities, for his nature refers to what he is like rather than who he is.'

171   On this see Richard B. Gaffin Jr, *By Faith not by Sight* (New Jersey: Presbyterian and Reformed, second edition 2013), 49.

172   Louth, 'The Place of Theosis', 35.

173   J. Todd Billings, *Calvin, Participation and the Gift: The Activity of Believers in Union with Christ* (Oxford: Oxford University, 2007), 63.

174   Calvin uses the idea of the 'energies' of God but for him they are not vague but related to the work of Jesus Christ and reaching us through the Holy Spirit. See Michael Horton, 'Calvin's Eucharistic Ecclesiology' in *Tributes to John Calvin: A Celebration of*

His Quincentenary, edited by David W. Hall (Phillipsburg: Presbyterian and Reformed, 2010).

175   Billings, *Calvin, Participation and the Gift*, 65.

176   Ibid., 67.

177   John Calvin, *Institutes of the Christian Religion*, ed. John T. McNeil, trans. Ford Lewis Battles (Louisville: Westminster John Knox, 1960), 3.11.22.

178   Kallistos Ware, *How are we Saved: The Understanding of Salvation in the Orthodox Tradition* (Minneapolis: Light and Life Publishing, 1996). In this chapter I will quote extensively the book. Instead of endnotes then I will put in parenthesis the pertinent page number.

179   Russell, *Fellow Workers,* 21.

180   Donald Fairbairn, *Grace and Christology in the Early Church, Oxford Early Christian Studies* (Oxford: Oxford University, 2006), 17-21.

181   Calvin, *Institutes*, 3.11.1.

182   Here we must also make reference to the 'future tense' of salvation which pertains to the redemption from the presence of sin in our world and lives.

183   Lossky, *Mystical Theology*, 202.

184   Ibid., 196.

185   Ibid., 197.

186   David Bentley Hart, 'Nor Height Nor Depth: On Toll Houses' in *Public Orthodoxy* (https://publicorthodoxy.org/tag/david-bentley-hart/).

187   Seraphim Rose, *The Soul After Death* (Saint Herman of Alaska Brotherhood, 1998).

188   Metropolitan Hierotheos Vlahos, *Life after Death* (Holy Monastery of the Birth of Theotokos, 2009).

189   This idea is fully argued and developed by Ronald K. Rittgers, 'The Age of Reform as an Age of Consolation', *Church History* 86 (2017), 607–42.

ALSO AVAILABLE IN THE *CHRISTIAN'S POCKET GUIDE* SERIES...

A Christian's Pocket Guide to Humanity

David McKay

The reality of being made in the image of God, but of being marred by sin, is the chief characteristic of the human race. This separation from our Creator, and ultimate union with him through the death of his Son affects all aspects of our lives. The issue of identity and the value of human life have come to the fore in recent years and David McKay's short book reminds us of who God has created us to be.

... a fine, clear summary of the salient points of biblical anthropology, integrating the doctrine into the broader context of creation, of the covenants and of Christology and salvation.

Carl R. Trueman
Professor of Biblical and Religious Studies,
Grove City College, Pennsylvania

978-1-5271-0640-6

A Christian's Pocket Guide to the Papacy

Leonardo DeChirico

Who are the Popes and how does the Roman Catholic Church define their role? What about the present day Popes? What is the ecumenical significance of the Papacy and what are its prospects in the global world? These and other questions are tackled as Leonardo De Chirico explores the Biblical, historical, and theological fabric of the Papacy.

In terms of an introduction to the Catholic Church's doctrine and exercise of the papacy, this book is unmatched! Read this book and you will gain essential insights into what for many Christians is a mystery, now unpacked by a trusted evangelical theologian and pastor.

Gregg R. Allison
Professor of Christian Theology, The Southern Baptist Theological Seminary, Louisville, Kentucky

978-1-7819-1299-7

A Christian's Pocket Guide to Loving the Old
Testament

Alec Motyer

Many of us know and love the stories and characters of
the Old Testament such as Joseph, Moses and Jonah.
But how do we view its importance in relation to New
Testament teaching and our 21st century experiences?
This accessible yet powerful addition to the Pocket Guide
series draw together the threads of Scripture to help us
understand the power of God's word when viewed in its
completeness.

*...If the world is still here in a hundred years' time, these
thrilling pages will still be looked upon as a treasure trove
among God's faithful people.*

Richard Bewes, OBE (1939 – 2019)
Formerly of All Souls Church, Langham Place,
London, England

978-1-7819-1580-6

A Christian's Pocket Guide to How We Got the
Bible

Greg Lanier

This short book answers some critical questions about
the Word of God, helping us to understand where
the Scriptures came from and why we can trust them.
Covering the origins and translations of the Old and
New Testaments, this straightforward introduction
answers many questions, and provides suggestions for
further reading if you want to research the topic further.

*Without being overly wordy or technical, this pocket guide
provides clear and accessible explanations for why we can be
confident that our Bibles are the Word of God.*

Nancy Guthrie
Bible teacher and author of *Seeing Jesus in the Old
Testament* series

978-1-5271-0268-2

A Christian's Pocket Guide to How God
Preserved the Bible

Richard Brash

There is sometimes a gap in the teaching we receive
between the inspiration and illumination of Scripture.
The Holy Spirit inspired the writing of the Word of God
in the first place and applies it to our hearts now. How do
we know that the Bible we read today is still the inspired
Word of God? Richard Brash grounds his answers to
these questions in the doctrines of God and His outer
works, especially providence, in this introductory guide
to how God preserved the Bible.

*This is a wonderfully lucid introduction to a much–neglected
doctrine. It will help many to grow in their confidence in the
Bible and in their adoration in the sovereign, speaking God.*

Vaughan Roberts
Rector of St Ebbe's, Oxford and Director of
Proclamation Trust

978-1-5271-0421-1

A Christian's Pocket Guide to Understanding
Suicide and Euthanasia

D. Eryl Davies

In a society that does not like to speak about death,
Eryl Davies brings a contemporary, biblical, pastoral
perspective on one of the most controversial topics of our
times. The desire to control when and how one's life ends
can be a complex and heart-breaking issue, so Davies
encourages Christians to be informed, and to engage
with the debate, bringing God's light to the darkness.

*… will be of great value to those needing immediate guidance
in difficult situations, as well as those who want to start
thinking more deeply about the issues raised by the current
debates on assisted dying, euthanasia and suicide.*

John Alcolado
Executive Dean, Chester Medical School, University of
Chester, UK

978-1-5271-0420-4

A Christian's Pocket Guide to Suffering
Brian H. Cosby

When tragedy strikes-the death of a child, hurricanes, a school shooting-we begin looking for an escape from the pain, a way out, or we clamor for answers from a panel of religious 'experts' to explain the ever-present question, 'Why?' We want answers and we want to believe that our suffering isn't meaningless.

A concisely written, pastorally focused, gospel-infused account of the place of suffering in the Christian life. A perfect guide to aid troubled souls find peace and comfort when the storm breaks.

Derek W. H. Thomas
Senior Minister of Preaching and Teaching,
First Presbyterian Church, Columbia, South Carolina

978-1-7819-1646-9

A Christian Pocket Guide to Mary
Leonardo De Chirico

A Christian's Pocket Guide to Mary offers a biblical account of Mary's character, contrasting this with the Roman Catholic traditions which have developed throughout history, distorting her nature from an obedient servant and worshipper of God to a worshipped saint herself. De Chirico writes with the authority of thorough research as well as personal experience of the traditions surrounding Mary which have become so integral to Roman Catholic worship.

Leonardo De Chirico is one of my most trusted authorities on Roman Catholic doctrine.... In this short book he demonstrates what the Roman Catholic Church teaches about Mary and aptly proves why so much of it is opposed to the plain teaching of the Bible. I heartily commend it to you.

Tim Challies
Blogger at www.challies.com

978-1-5271-0060-2

Christian Focus Publications

Our mission statement —

STAYING FAITHFUL

In dependence upon God we seek to impact the world through literature faithful to His infallible Word, the Bible. Our aim is to ensure that the Lord Jesus Christ is presented as the only hope to obtain forgiveness of sin, live a useful life and look forward to heaven with Him.

Our books are published in four imprints:

CHRISTIAN
FOCUS

Popular works including biographies, commentaries, basic doctrine and Christian living.

CHRISTIAN
HERITAGE

Books representing some of the best material from the rich heritage of the church.

MENTOR

Books written at a level suitable for Bible College and seminary students, pastors, and other serious readers. The imprint includes commentaries, doctrinal studies, examination of current issues and church history.

CF4•K

Children's books for quality Bible teaching and for all age groups: Sunday school curriculum, puzzle and activity books; personal and family devotional titles, biographies and inspirational stories — because you are never too young to know Jesus!

Christian Focus Publications Ltd,
Geanies House, Fearn, Ross-shire,
IV20 1TW, Scotland, United Kingdom.
www.christianfocus.com